I Modify IKEA®

I Modify IKEA®

Furnishings from Everyone's Favorite Store, Customized for Your Home

Elyse Major & Charlotte Rivers

Ulysses Press

This book is not associated with or authorized or approved by IKEA®

A QUINTET BOOK

Copyright © 2016
Quintet Publishing Limited

Published in the US by
ULYSSES PRESS
PO Box 3440
Berkeley, CA 94703
www.ulyssespress.com

ISBN 978-1-61243-610-4
Library of Congress Control Number: 2016934484

First published in 2016 in the United Kingdom as *50 Flatpack Hacks* by Quintet Publishing Limited

Managing Editor: Cheryl Brown
Senior Editor: Caroline Elliker
Designer: Luke Herriott
Art Director: Mark Hudson
Publisher: Mark Searle

Photographers: Marisa Bettencourt (mstudiosri.com/marisa) pages 36, 37, 82, 84, 85; Rachel Denbow: page 16; Sarah M. Dorsey: pages 90, 91; Jane Hughes: pages 2, 60, 106, 107, 127; Jenni Juurinen: pages 100, 114, 131, 133; Stephanie Jones: pages 96, 110; Elyse Major: pages 13, 15, 23, 24, 27, 38, 43, 74, 78, 80, 105, 121, 135; Jessica Mayhall: pages 69, 70, 72; Audrey Smit: pages 94, 137; Iris Thorsteinsdottir (www.iristhors.com) pages 10, 18, 21, 28, 30, 31, 34, 40, 44, 49, 51, 54, 56, 58, 62, 64, 65, 88, 103, 112, 116, 117, 118, 122, 123, 140.

While every effort has been made to credit photographers, the publisher would like to apologize should there have been any omissions or errors, and would be pleased to make the appropriate correction for future editions of the book.

Cover designed and illustrated by what!design@whatweb.com

Manufactured in China by 1010 Printing International Ltd.

9 8 7 6 5 4 3 2 1

CONTENTS

PROJECT SELECTOR

UNIQUE TOUCHES

PAGE 12
MAIL ORGANIZER

PAGE 14
TABLE LAMP

PAGE 16
STRAW BUNTING

PAGE 18
LED CANDLES

PAGE 20
TEALIGHT HOLDERS

PAGE 22
FABRIC-COVERED
COASTERS

PAGE 24
THROW PILLOWS:
SHAM PILLOW

PAGE 26
THROW PILLOWS:
APPLIQUÉ PILLOW

PAGE 28
BOOK LEDGES:
SCALLOPS

PAGE 30
BOOK LEDGES:
POLKA DOTS

PAGE 31
FABRIC LAMPSHADE

PAGE 34
PAINTED CUSHIONS

PAGE 36
ROLLER BLIND

PAGE 38
DISH TOWEL

PAGE 40
DECKING BATHMAT

PAGE 42
COLORFUL DECKING

PAGE 44
SHOWER CURTAIN

PAGE 48
BASKET LIGHTSHADE

PAGE 50
PICNIC BASKET

PAGE 54
PICNIC THROW

STORAGE SOLUTIONS

PAGE 56
FLOWER POTS

PAGE 60
PLANTER BOXES

PAGE 62
STORAGE BASKETS

PAGE 64
JEWELRY BOX

PAGE 68
COPPER SHELVING

INTRODUCTION

All around the world, people are picking up paint-brushes and power tools and turning affordable, mass-produced furniture into décor that is at once personal, unique, and stylish. Propelled by the do-it-yourself and upcycling movement, and the abundance of print and online inspiration, many of us are feeling emboldened to try modifying furniture.

Flatpack furniture, furnishings that are sold in pieces requiring customer assembly, is ideal for transformation because of its winning combination of affordability, contemporary design, and clean lines—not to mention its pre-fab portability! With self-assembly fixtures, there isn't the pressure of ruining a treasured heirloom, and the typically smooth surfaces lend themselves to adhering paper, stenciling designs, adding appliqués, paint finishes, and more. Like decorative stepping stones, flatpack furniture offers a sturdy springboard primed and ready for taking leaps.

Modifying self-assembly furniture is also known as a flatpack hack. Both the terms "flatpack" and "hack" are relatively new to us. Flatpack describes an object that requires self-assembly and is packed flat, and it is this type of furniture that the phenomonal success of IKEA® home furnishings has been built on (the company credits this innovation to an early employee needing to remove the legs of a table to fit into his car). The first IKEA® home furnishings store opened in Sweden in 1958; today, it is the world's largest furniture retailer with more than 300 stores worldwide.

Through the years, "hack" has implied everything from a terrible writer to what happens when someone breaks into a computer network, although somehow it has been co-opted along the way into meaning a

clever modification. For many furniture hackers, the process begins with sizing up possibilities. Could that basket work as a lampshade? What if I turned this bookcase onto its side? How would it look in metallic?

In this book, coauthors Elyse Major and Charlotte Rivers, along with a host of contributing makers, were given the task of reworking self-assembly furniture and related home accents with structural and ornamental twists. The book is divided into three categories: Unique Touches, Storage Solutions, and Functional Fun. Within these sections, there are projects in three skill levels from basic to advanced. A "basic" modification might require only scissors and glue. For best results, carefully review a project before starting, noting the supplies and tools, and getting a sense of the time and space you might need.

Each project in the book offers illustrations and step-by-step instructions to re-create the examples shown, or hack the hacks and make them uniquely your own. As with almost any type of project, even following directions closely can lead to a slightly different outcome, simply by the nature of our preferences, abilities, and techniques. For example, while the Pantry Cupboard project (see page 84) has been outfitted with a cottage-style sensibility, you may wish to switch out the faded florals for a vibrant graphic print, and opt for a shiny bright lacquer over a distressed paint finish. The projects presented are all meant to be very adaptable and we have worked very hard to present fresh ideas.

The aim of this book is to show how basic designs can be customized to fit your life, style, and space. It's all about thinking outside the cardboard box.

PRODUCT AVAILABILITY

All the contributing makers have used IKEA® home furnishings products as the start point for their modifications, and we have provided details of the models they have used. On occasion some of these may have been discontinued, or may no longer be available in a particular territory. In such cases, a search on eBay may reveal the exact item you require, or often an alternative IKEA® home furnishings product can be sourced from www.ikea.com. We encourage you to apply the ideas to items you own, wherever you may have sourced them from.

Please note: All prices provided were correct when preparing copy for publication (February 2016).

UNIQUE TOUCHES

FULL OF QUICK, EASY PROJECTS YOU CAN PUT
TOGETHER IN NO TIME, THIS CHAPTER PROVIDES
INSPIRATION FOR ALL THOSE WHO WANT TO MAKE
A BIG DIFFERENCE TO THEIR HOME WITHOUT
SPENDING MUCH OR WORKING TOO HARD.
THESE UNIQUE LITTLE TOUCHES ARE FULL
OF PERSONALITY AND FUN!

MAIL ORGANIZER

Designed by: Elyse Major

Too sturdy and decorative for napkins alone, mount the
LIKSIDIG napkin holder to the wall to keep letters handy.
Create and hang many for a clever and organized display or
use small, strong magnets to hang memos from the front.

MATERIALS

IKEA® HOME FURNISHINGS **LIKSIDIG**
NAPKIN HOLDER
WHITE, $3.99

- **SPRAY PAINT**
- **MOUNTING HARDWARE,
  HEAVY-DUTY MOUNTING TAPE, OR PUTTY**

TIME: 30 MINS
DIFFICULTY: BASIC

HACK HINT: Enhance the look by
painting the leaves and rose motifs
in different colors.

INSTRUCTIONS

1 Lay down newspaper to prepare an area
outdoors for spray-painting. Prop the napkin
holder up on a brick, tin cans, or something
similar to allow for easy access to all sides.

2 Spray-paint the napkin holder with a waving
motion to cover the piece. (Follow the
manufacturer's instructions for best spray-
painting results.) Apply additional coats if
needed; allow it to dry thoroughly.

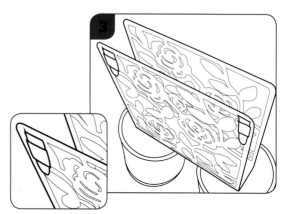

3 Install mounting hardware, mounting tape,
or putty to one side of the mail organizer,
following the manufacturer's guidelines.

TABLE LAMP

Designed by: Elyse Major

Give this low-cost lamp high-end style by adorning
it with an artificial flower and a bold, metallic finish.
It will add a touch of shine to any room.

MATERIALS

IKEA® HOME FURNISHINGS **LAMPAN**
TABLE LAMP
ANY COLOR, $4.99

IKEA® HOME FURNISHINGS **SMYCKA**
ARTIFICIAL CHRYSANTHEMUM FLOWER
ASSORTED COLORS, $0.99

- **SHARP SCISSORS OR CLIPPING TOOL**
- **HOT GLUE GUN WITH GLUE**
- **RUST-OLEUM BRIGHT COAT SPRAY PAINT IN METALLIC FINISH**

TIME: 30–60 MINS
DIFFICULTY: BASIC

INSTRUCTIONS

1 Remove any product stickers from the lamp and dust away any debris.

2 Use sharp scissors or a clipping tool to cut the bloom from its stem, making sure to keep the bloom intact. Using a hot glue gun with glue, attach the flower to the lampshade. Press firmly to ensure it is set, being careful of the hot glue.

3 Cover the cording. (For the finished project as shown, it has been covered with a plastic bag, but paper or low-tack tape could also be used.)

4 Lay down newspaper to prepare an area outdoors for spray-painting. Spray-paint the entire lamp, including the flower. (Follow the manufacturer's instructions for best spray-painting results.) Allow the lamp to dry well. Repeat to give additional coat(s) of spray paint, if desired.

STRAW BUNTING

Designed by: Rachel Denbow

This quick and easy tutorial transforms a box of
SOMMAFINT straws into colorful bunting that's
ideal to brighten up a child's bedroom.

MATERIALS

IKEA® HOME FURNISHINGS **SOMMAFINT** STRAWS
ASSORTED COLORS, $1.49/100 PACK

- **TWINE, EMBROIDERY THREAD,
  OR THIN ROPE**
- **SCISSORS**

TIME: 30 MINS
DIFFICULTY: BASIC

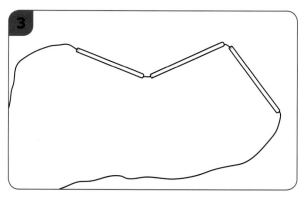

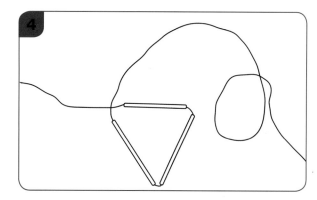

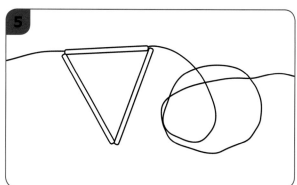

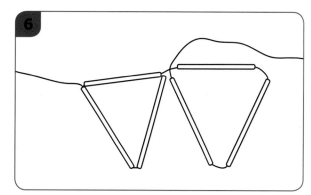

INSTRUCTIONS

1 Decide how long you want your bunting to be and multiply by three to get your twine length. Pink twine is used here, but you could also use embroidery thread or thin rope.

2 You will need three straws to make each triangle. Cut down all the straws you need to 6 inches (15 cm) in length.

3 Place the first three straws onto your twine and push them to about 6 inches (15 cm) before the end of the twine.

4 Move the twine around to arrange the three straws into a triangle shape.

5 Take the long end of your twine and pass it back through the top straw, as shown.

6 Add three straws in the same order of size/color and restring the long end of the twine through the top to make your next triangle.

7 To complete the bunting, continue to make triangles in the same way until you fill the length of your twine.

LED CANDLES

Designed by: Charlotte Rivers

Use permanent markers in three different colors to create a series of simple, striking patterns on a set of **STÖPEN** LED candles. It's so easy to personalize the designs by selecting any colors or patterns that you like.

MATERIALS

IKEA® HOME FURNISHINGS **STÖPEN**
LED BLOCK CANDLES
WHITE, BATTERY OPERATED, $9.99/SET OF 3

- **3 PERMANENT MARKERS**

TIME: 1 HR
DIFFICULTY: BASIC

HACK HINT: You may need to go over each shape two or three times with the marker to make sure the colors are bold enough.

INSTRUCTIONS

1 Three different patterns were created for these candles: triangles, scallops, and sprinkles. This is a freehand project, so it is a good idea to do a trial run on paper first to perfect your shapes before you apply your marker to the candles.

2 Once you are confident with your shapes, you can begin. Start by drawing a line of small triangles on the middle-sized candle using a black marker.

3 Build up the amount of shapes around each LED candle to create a random pattern, as shown.

4 Once finished, move on to the tallest candle and build up a pattern of scallop shapes using a blue marker.

5 Finally, draw a pretty sprinkle pattern on the smallest candle in yellow marker.

TEALIGHT HOLDERS

Designed by: Charlotte Rivers

For this project, take a pair of tealight holders and cover them in gold leaf. Adding gold leaf is a great way to make an item look instantly sophisticated.

MATERIALS

IKEA® HOME FURNISHINGS **GLASIG**
TEALIGHT HOLDERS
CLEAR GLASS, $2.99/5 PACK

- **GOLD LEAF KIT WITH GLUE AND GLUE APPLICATOR**
- **CRAFT KNIFE**
- **PAINTBRUSH**

TIME: 1 HR
DIFFICULTY: BASIC

HACK HINT: When applying gold leaf, make sure your hands are clean and dry. Wash off any glue as you go to avoid the leaf sticking to your fingers.

INSTRUCTIONS

1 First cut the gold leaf into pieces that are of a manageable size using a craft knife. Here, the gold leaf is cut to the depth of the tealight holder.

2 Apply the glue (supplied with the gold leaf kit) to the outside of the tealight holder. Apply a small amount at a time, just as much as you need for the first piece of leaf you are going to apply.

3 Now start to apply your gold leaf to the tealight holder, one small piece at a time. Handle the leaf carefully and press very gently to secure it to the glass. Do not press or rub too hard, as this will tear the leaf.

4 Continue applying gold leaf around each tealight holder. You can use a paintbrush to lightly rub the leaf onto the glass as you go.

FABRIC-COVERED COASTERS

Designed by: Elyse Major

Dot the room with pops of pattern while protecting your surfaces with these easy-to-makeover coasters. For a coordinating pillow project, see Appliqué Pillow, page 26.

MATERIALS

IKEA® HOME FURNISHINGS **ÖNSKEDRÖM** COASTERS
ASSORTED PATTERNS, $0.99/10 PACK

IKEA® HOME FURNISHINGS **ROSMARIE** FABRIC
WHITE AND GRAY, $8.99/YARD

- **WHITE COPIER PAPER**
- **PENCIL**
- **SHARP SCISSORS**
- **GLUE STICK**
- **FOAM BRUSH**
- **DECOUPAGE GLUE/SEALER SUCH AS MOD PODGE**

TIME: 30 MINS
DIFFICULTY: BASIC

INSTRUCTIONS

1 Begin by turning each coaster into a blank canvas by covering the design side with a circle of white paper. To cut four circles at once, fold one sheet of standard copier paper into four, crease well and place a coaster in the center; trace around the coaster with a pencil and carefully cut out through all folds. Repeat as required.

2 Using a light application of glue stick, affix one plain circle to the top of each coaster. Press gently to smooth.

3 Using a coaster as a template, trace and cut circles from pressed fabric. Affix over the plain circle using the glue stick.

4 Using a dry foam brush, apply a smooth, light coating of decoupage glue/sealer to the entire top surface of each coaster. Allow it to dry and repeat.

HACK HINT: Flat, ironed fabric will work best for this project.

THROW PILLOWS

Designed by: Elyse Major

Add instant panache to plain pillows with these no-sew ideas:
fold a duvet pillowcase into a square or add a strip of alluring fabric
to an existing cover. Scatter about for effortless sophistication.

MATERIALS

IKEA® HOME FURNISHINGS **ULLKAKTUS** PILLOW WHITE, $3.99

IKEA® HOME FURNISHINGS **ALVINE KVIST** DUVET COVER AND PILLOWCASE SET WHITE AND GRAY, $29.99

- **FABRIC ADHESIVE: UNIQUE STITCH**
- **APPLIQUÉ FASTENER**

TIME: 30 MINS
DIFFICULTY: BASIC

INSTRUCTIONS: SHAM PILLOW

1 Insert the pillow deep into the duvet pillowcase so that it sits at the bottom.

2 Fold the empty top section of the pillowcase over, button-side up. Position so that it looks like it was made for this smaller-sized insert.

3 Draw lines of fabric adhesive onto the reverse of the appliqué fastener and position to secure the flap. Press gently to secure. Allow it to set and dry.

INSTRUCTIONS: APPLIQUÉ PILLOW

1 Using the **ULLKAKTUS** or a similar pillow as your guide, determine the size of the area you wish to cover. You could use a narrow strip, a square, or a wide strip of fabric, as shown.

2 If you prefer a frayed edge, as shown, snip and gently tear the fabric; if you prefer a clean edge then cut with scissors or a rotary cutter.

3 Determine how you wish to position the fabric on the pillow. Draw a thin line of fabric adhesive to the reverse of the fabric (see detail below). Smudge it with your finger so that a glue line won't be visible through the fabric on the finished pillow.

4 Carefully position the fabric section, glue-side down; gently press and smooth, and wipe away any glue smudges. Allow it to set and dry prior to use.

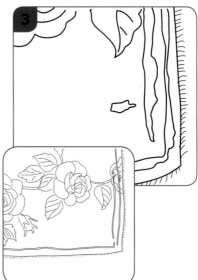
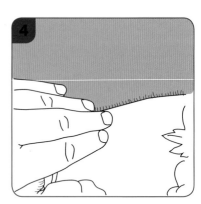

MATERIALS

IKEA® HOME FURNISHINGS **ULLKAKTUS** PILLOW GRAY, $3.99

IKEA® HOME FURNISHINGS **ROSMARIE** FABRIC WHITE AND GRAY, $8.99/YARD

- **SHARP SCISSORS OR ROTARY CUTTER**
- **FABRIC ADHESIVE: UNIQUE STITCH**

TIME: 30 MINS
DIFFICULTY: BASIC

BOOK LEDGES

Designed by: Charlotte Rivers

The **MOSSLANDA** picture ledge makes a really great children's bookshelf as it allows you to store books with the covers facing forward. It comes in two sizes; this hack uses the larger one. There are two decorative motifs for you to choose from— scallops or polka dots.

MATERIALS

IKEA® HOME FURNISHINGS
MOSSLANDA PICTURE LEDGE
WHITE, 45¼ INCHES (115 CM),
$9.99

- **CONTACT PAPER**
- **CIRCLE CUTTER**
- **CRAFT MAT**
- **RULER**
- **CRAFT KNIFE**
- **WASHI OR MASKING TAPE**

TIME: 1 HR
DIFFICULTY: BASIC

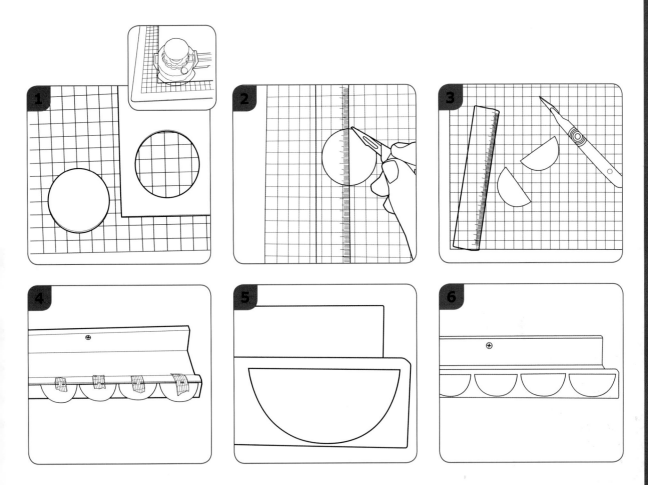

INSTRUCTIONS: SCALLOPS

1 Take your contact paper—in this case black—and begin by using your circle cutter to cut a circle out of the contact paper. Ensure that it measures 2 inches (5 cm) in diameter. Repeat until you have 11 circles.

2 Use your craft mat to position your contact paper circle (right side down) in the middle of a 2 x 2 inch (5 x 5 cm) grid. Using a craft knife and ruler, cut the circle in half down the center to create two scallop shapes.

3 Repeat with all your circles. Once completed you should have 22 scallop shapes.

4 Now to apply the scallop shapes to your ledge. Instead of sticking them straight onto the ledge, it is best to test the positioning of them first using washi or masking tape, to ensure that they are evenly spaced along your ledge. Placing the scallops a small distance apart along the ledge should result in an even spread, but adjust if necessary.

5 Once you are happy with the spacing, start at one end and stick each scallop in place, leaving an equal gap at top and bottom.

6 Continue until all 22 scallop shapes have been applied.

MATERIALS

IKEA® HOME FURNISHINGS **MOSSLANDA**
PICTURE LEDGE
WHITE, 45¼ INCHES (115 CM), $9.99

- **CONTACT PAPER, ASSORTED COLORS**
- **HOLE PUNCH**

TIME: 1 HR
DIFFICULTY: BASIC

INSTRUCTIONS: POLKA DOTS

1 Take your contact papers—in this case yellow, orange, and pink—and use a hole punch to cut out lots of little multicolored contact paper dots.

2 Simply stick your multicolored contact paper dots randomly along one edge of the shelf.

FABRIC LAMPSHADE

Designed by: Charlotte Rivers

This project sees the classic **JÄRA** lampshade wrapped in a length of subtle, leafy fabric. A different patterned or plain fabric could be used, depending on the color scheme of your bedroom.

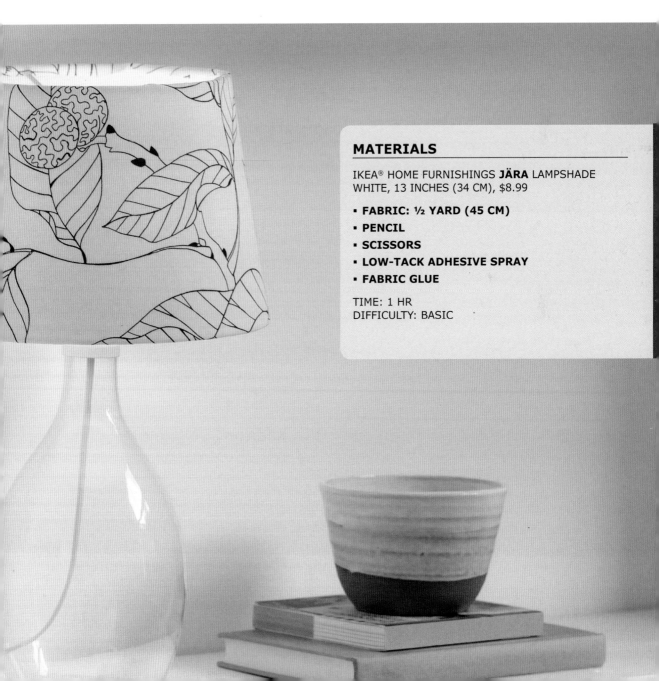

MATERIALS

IKEA® HOME FURNISHINGS **JÄRA** LAMPSHADE WHITE, 13 INCHES (34 CM), $8.99

- **FABRIC: ½ YARD (45 CM)**
- **PENCIL**
- **SCISSORS**
- **LOW-TACK ADHESIVE SPRAY**
- **FABRIC GLUE**

TIME: 1 HR
DIFFICULTY: BASIC

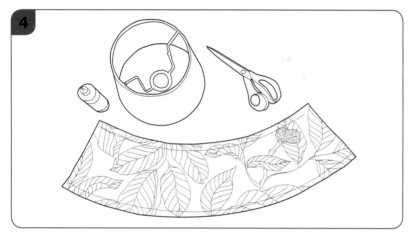

INSTRUCTIONS

1 This lampshade is slightly cone shaped (as opposed to straight) so you will need a curved piece of material to cover it. To work out the shape, lay your fabric out on a clean, flat surface, right side down, and place your lampshade on top of it. Then, using a pencil, start to roll the lampshade along, while at the same time drawing a line alongside the rolling shade onto the fabric.

2 Starting at the bottom, draw a line one way, and then change direction and draw a line the other way, this time in line with the top edge. Make sure you roll the lampshade in one continuous movement each way, without lifting or moving the lampshade up or down. You will end up with two lines on your fabric.

3 Now you are ready to cut your fabric. Using your drawn lines as a guide, begin cutting your fabric, leaving an allowance of 3/8 inch (1 cm) on either side of the lines at the top and bottom. This excess fabric will be folded into the shade to give you a neat edge.

4 Once your fabric is cut out, you are ready to cover your shade with it. Lay the fabric out flat (right side down) and spray evenly with low-tack adhesive spray.

HACK HINT: If the fabric you have chosen has a directional pattern, ensure it is facing the right way before you begin to mark and cut out your lampshade shape.

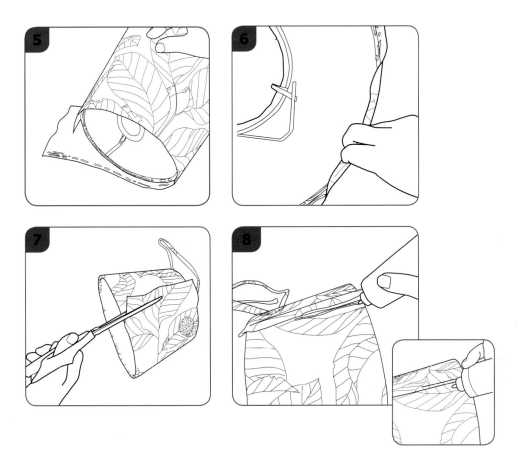

5 Place the shade onto the fabric—line up the top and bottom with your pencil lines—and then roll the shade along the fabric, keeping it in line with your drawn lines. Adjust the fabric as you roll (if necessary) to ensure that there is an even amount of excess fabric at the top and bottom of the shade.

6 Once the fabric is wrapped and secured with the low-tack adhesive, you can apply fabric glue to the rim of the shade and begin to fold the excess fabric into the rim. Do this at the top and the bottom.

7 Once all your fabric is folded in and secured, trim away any excess fabric you may have at your join area.

8 Apply a line of fabric glue along the bottom side of the join. Fold the top piece of fabric over, apply fabric glue to the underside of the fold, and then press together to secure the folded join in place. Allow the lampshade to dry.

HACK HINT: When you roll the fabric around the shade, try to start the fabric rolling process at the same point as the join in your uncovered shade. That way the fabric join will sit in the same place, and only one join will be visible when the lamp is on.

PAINTED CUSHIONS

Designed by: Charlotte Rivers

This simple white cushion cover is ideal for customization, allowing you to add a personal touch to it to create a unique look for your bedroom.

VARIATION

Why not try a different shape? For the cushion pictured on the right, another grid has been created using a scallop and dot pattern. To do this, follow Steps 1–6, finding something circular to draw around to create your scallop template, and then apply your paint to the marked-out shapes.

MATERIALS

IKEA® HOME FURNISHINGS **GURLI** CUSHION COVERS WHITE, $4.00 EACH

- **IRON AND IRONING BOARD**
- **PAPER**
- **PENCIL**
- **RULER**
- **CARD STOCK**
- **SCISSORS**
- **FABRIC PAINT**
- **PAINTBRUSH**

TIME: 1 HR
DIFFICULTY: BASIC

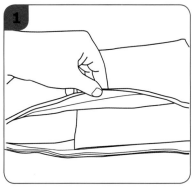

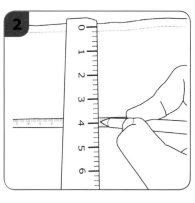

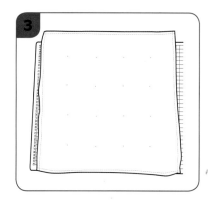

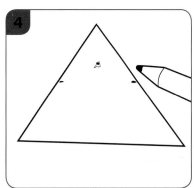

INSTRUCTIONS

1 Wash and iron the cushion cover. Before you begin to paint, line the inside of the cover with sheets of paper to ensure that the paint does not seep through to the back of the cushion as you decorate it.

2 Next, mark out a grid so you know where to paint the triangle shapes. The cushion measures 20 x 20 inches (51 x 51 cm), so start by measuring 4 inches (10 cm) in and 4 inches (10 cm) down from the top left corner. Mark this point lightly with a pencil.

3 Keep moving along 4 inches (10 cm) and marking 4 inches (10 cm) down until you reach the end of the row. Repeat for another three rows until you have a grid of 16 dots marked out.

4 Cut out a triangle-shaped piece of card stock. Make two level marks on each side to form a guide as to how long your triangle shape should be, and then make a hole in the middle. The marks and the hole will help you to position your triangles centrally and ensure that they are all the same size.

5 Place your card guide over the first dot on the grid, positioning the hole over the penciled dot. Draw a light pencil line up and down each side of the card guide to your desired (marked) length. Repeat until you have 16 shapes drawn, then rub out the penciled dots.

6 Take your paintbrush and paint over the marked shapes with fabric paint. Once dry, iron the cover to heat-set the fabric paint.

ROLLER BLIND

Designed by: Elyse Major

Easily upgrade white roller blinds from basic to custom with the addition of colored stripes. Painter's or washi tape is available in a myriad of colors and patterns, so you can make a new look for every room.

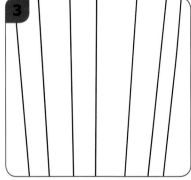

MATERIALS

IKEA® HOME FURNISHINGS **TUPPLUR**
ROLLER BLIND
BLOCK-OUT, WHITE, $23.99

- **RULER**
- **SCISSORS**
- **GREEN OR BLUE FROGTAPE MULTI-SURFACE PAINTER'S TAPE, OR WASHI TAPE**

TIME: 30 MINS
DIFFICULTY: BASIC

INSTRUCTIONS

1 Prior to hanging your blind, lay it flat on a table or smooth work surface and unfurl as far as you plan to ever extend it.

2 Determine a starting point for your stripe (at the edge of the fabric, or the width of the tape from the fabric edge), cut a piece of tape the entire length, and carefully position it onto the fabric, using a ruler as a guide.

3 Continue adding stripes of tape until you have the look you want: variations include vertical or horizontal stripes, narrow or wide, or adding horizontal lines over vertical lines to create a plaid.

HACK HINT: If you are using low-tack tape, it won't be difficult to reposition if needed, but still take care when removing it to avoid tears.

DISH TOWEL

Designed by: Stacey Remiker-Flesch

Create a folkloric-inspired, embellished dish towel with the simple addition of pretty patterned flowers and leaves.

MATERIALS

IKEA® HOME FURNISHINGS **TEKLA** DISH TOWEL WHITE, RED, $0.79

- **FLOWER AND LEAF TEMPLATE**
- **PRINTER AND PAPER**
- **SCISSORS**
- **PAPER-BACKED FUSIBLE WEB: PELLON WONDER-UNDER 805**
- **FABRIC SCRAPS**
- **IRON**
- **PENCIL**
- **WATER-SOLUBLE FABRIC PEN/MARKER (OPTIONAL)**
- **EMBROIDERY NEEDLE**
- **GREEN EMBROIDERY THREAD**

TIME: 1 HR+
DIFFICULTY: INTERMEDIATE

Flower and Leaf Template

HACK HINT: Re-trace template shapes onto card stock paper for sturdier, reusable template pattern pieces.

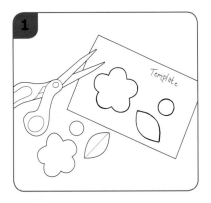

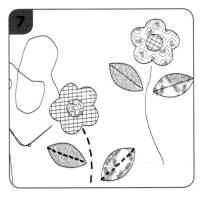

INSTRUCTIONS

1 Begin by tracing a copy of the flower and leaf template. Cut out each individual shape.

2 Cut out fusible web pieces large enough to cover the back of the fabric scrap pieces. Iron the fusible web pieces onto the reverse of each fabric scrap, following the manufacturer's instructions.

3 Use the templates and a pencil to trace the shapes onto the reverse side (paper side) of the fabric pieces (two flower shapes, two flower centers, and four leaves in total), and cut out each shape.

4 Peel off the paper backing on each cut shape. Place the flower and leaf shapes fabric face up on the right side of the towel (see photo opposite for layout).

5 Press over the fabric pieces with an iron to fuse them to the dish towel.

6 Use the water-soluble marker to draw a stem for each flower and a "vein" down the center of each leaf. Alternatively, stitch the stems and leaf veins freehand without marking the towel.

7 Using green embroidery thread and an embroidery needle, add a simple running stitch to create your stems and leaf veins.

8 Lastly, with embroidery thread and needle, hand-stitch around each fabric shape with an appliqué/whip stitch. This step can be omitted, but will provide a more finished appearance, while securely bonding the fabric to the dish towel.

DECKING BATHMAT

Designed by: Charlotte Rivers

This great little hack repurposes **RUNNEN** decking into a neat bathmat. The 12-square mat shown here is made using four sections of decking, but you could use more sections to make a bigger mat.

MATERIALS

IKEA® HOME FURNISHINGS
RUNNEN FLOOR DECKING
BROWN STAINED, $34.99/9 PACK

- **HACKSAW**

TIME: 45 MINS
DIFFICULTY: INTERMEDIATE

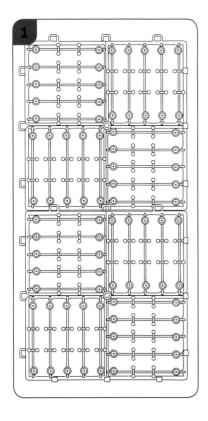

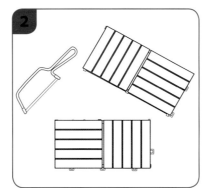

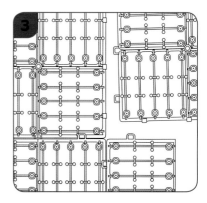

INSTRUCTIONS

1 Take two sections of decking and secure them together following the assembly instructions.

2 Take a third section of decking and saw it in half using a hacksaw.

3 Attach one of the sawn half sections to the first full section of decking. Then take a fourth section of decking and line it up with the rest of the mat so you can work out which way you need to saw it in half based on where the clips are. You can then cut that section in half as well.

4 Now you can add your final half piece to complete your mat.

5 Finally saw off any unwanted connectors from the edges of your completed mat.

HACK HINT: Be sure to work out exactly how the different sections will clip together before cutting any sections in half.

COLORFUL DECKING

Designed by: Elyse Major

Paint and connect colorful **SKOGHALL** decking squares to create a welcoming place for boots. Or why not use to line a wall or wrap a corner in vibrant color?

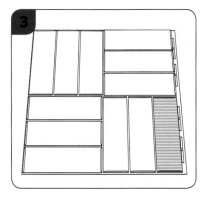

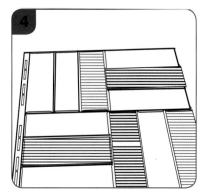

MATERIALS

IKEA® HOME FURNISHINGS **SKOGHALL** DECKING ACACIA, $24.99/10 PACK

- **WHITE SPRAY PAINT**
- **PAINT: LATEX, ACRYLIC CRAFT, ETC. IN ASSORTED COLORS**
- **SMALL, FLAT PAINTBRUSH**
- **DECOUPAGE GLUE/SEALER OR VARNISH (OPTIONAL)**

TIME: 30–60 MINS
DIFFICULTY: INTERMEDIATE

INSTRUCTIONS

1 Lay down newspaper to prepare an area outdoors for spray painting. Follow the manufacturer's instructions for best results. Prop each section up on a brick or similar to allow for easy access to the top and sides.

2 Apply a coat of white spray paint as primer to cover the dark wood, and set aside. Once dry, give a second coat, if needed.

3 Gather assorted colors of paint and begin to cover your sections. For best results use a small, flat paintbrush, which will allow you to lightly sweep between the grooves, if necessary.

4 Apply as many coats of paint as desired. Seal with decoupage glue/sealer or varnish, or leave unsealed to weather.

5 Once each piece has dried, follow the assembly instructions to connect the decking. A line of three sections is shown here, but you could also make a wider rectangle, an L-shape to wrap around corners, and more.

HACK HINT: The choice is yours whether to paint in a planned pattern or work in a random order, as shown here.

SHOWER CURTAIN

Designed by: Charlotte Rivers

This hack transforms the colorful **TOFSVIVA** duvet cover into a shower curtain that will brighten up any bathroom. A different duvet cover could be used to match your bathroom color scheme.

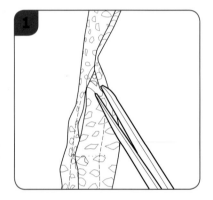

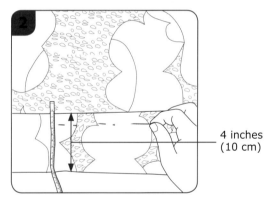

4 inches
(10 cm)

MATERIALS

IKEA® HOME FURNISHINGS **TOFSVIVA** DUVET SET MULTICOLOR, $29.99

- **SCISSORS OR SEAM RIPPER**
- **RULER OR TAPE MEASURE**
- **PINS**
- **IRON AND IRONING BOARD**
- **SEWING MACHINE**
- **NEEDLE AND THREAD**
- **CLEAR PLASTIC SHOWER CURTAIN LINER**
- **SET OF 12 SHOWER CURTAIN RINGS**

TIME: 3–4 HRS
DIFFICULTY: INTERMEDIATE

INSTRUCTIONS

1 Begin by using scissors or a seam ripper to unpick the stitching on the three sides of the duvet cover. The top is folded, so simply cut along the folded line to end up with two separate pieces of material.

2 Set one piece of material aside then lay out the other piece on a flat surface, right side down. Measure, fold, and pin a 4-inch (10-cm) hem on each of the four sides. Press the hems using an iron.

HACK HINT: You will end up with a spare piece of material. You could use this on another project, for instance, we have used it on the **KALLAX** Reading Bench project on page 88.

HACK HINT: Most sewing machines will have a marker to guide to sew a 3/8-inch (1-cm) straight line.

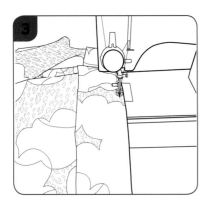
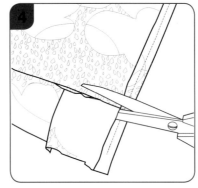

3 Now you are ready to sew. Begin by machine sewing a straight line, 3/8 inch (1 cm) in from the edge of the hem on each side edge of the shower curtain. Repeat to sew the top and bottom hems in the same way.

4 Cut away any excess fabric from the two side hems and the bottom hem. *Do not* cut away any fabric from the top hem.

HACK HINT: A sewing machine with a buttonhole function is useful but not essential.

5 For the top hem (where your shower curtain rings will be fitted), you need to fold, pin, and press an additional small 3/4-inch (2-cm) hem at the bottom of your 4-inch (10-cm) hem on the inside of your shower curtain. Sew along this hemline, 3/8 inch (1 cm) in from the edge of the hem.

6 Use your sewing machine's buttonhole function to make 12 buttonholes along the top hem, marking them up first: measure in 2 inches (5 cm), make a mark, then measure along 5½ inches (14 cm), make another mark, and continue until you have 12 marks. If you do not have a buttonhole function on your sewing machine, follow Steps 7–11.

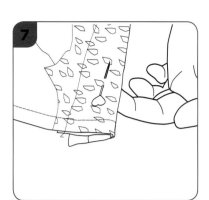
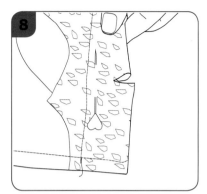
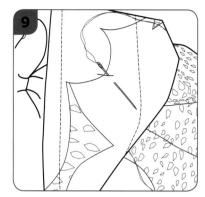

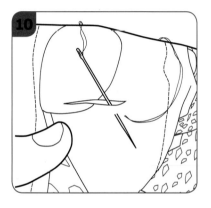
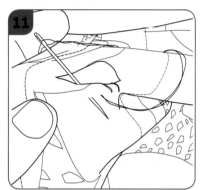

7 Turn the fabric over and fold the top hem in half on itself and secure it with pins.

8 Now cut a series of slits to create the holes for your curtain rings. Measure in 2 inches (5 cm) and make your first cut using your scissors. Cut ⅜ inch (1 cm) on the fold to give you a ¾-inch (2-cm) cut. Continue on along the fold making cuts every 5½ inches (14 cm). This will give you 12 holes.

9 Secure the edges of each hole with a needle and thread. Thread your needle, tie a knot in the end, and push the needle up through the fabric from the back.

10 Pass the needle though the hole and push it back up through the fabric. Pull the thread through and repeat.

11 Continue on around the hole until you are back at the starting point.

12 Now you are ready to hang your curtain together with the clear plastic shower curtain liner using your shower curtain rings.

BASKET LIGHTSHADE

Designed by: Charlotte Rivers

This is a nifty little hack that sees a wicker basket of your choice turned into a pendant lightshade for a bedroom. The best thing about using a basket is the pattern it creates on the ceiling when the light is on.

MATERIALS

IKEA® HOME FURNISHINGS **GADDIS** BASKET NATURAL, $4.99

- **SCISSORS**
- **SCREWDRIVER**

TIME: 45 MINS
DIFFICULTY: INTERMEDIATE

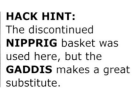

HACK HINT:
The discontinued **NIPPRIG** basket was used here, but the **GADDIS** makes a great substitute.

INSTRUCTIONS

1 Use a pair of scissors to work a small hole into the center of the base of the basket.

2 Twist the scissors around in the hole until it measures 3/8 inch (1 cm) wide.

3 Next, you will need to take your light fixture apart. First, make sure the main electrical switch to the lights in your house is *switched off* at the circuit breaker. Then you can remove the outer housing by unscrewing each end.

4 Take a small screwdriver and unscrew the little screws that hold the two wires into the light fixture.

5 Completely remove the wire from the fixture. Feed it through the hole that you made in the basket. You can then feed the wire back through the top part of the housing, secure the individual wires back into the fixture, and screw the bottom part of the housing back in position.

PICNIC BASKET

Designed by: Charlotte Rivers

Wrapping the handles in five complementary shades of soft yarn adds color and style to this lovely lightweight picnic basket. The addition of pom-poms—made from the leftover yarn—to one of the handles gives an extra-special finishing touch.

MATERIALS

WICKER PICNIC BASKET

- **FABRIC GLUE**
- **RULER OR TAPE MEASURE**
- **5 COLORS OF 100% COTTON YARN**
- **SCISSORS**
- **CARD STOCK OR POM-POM MAKER**

TIME: 1½ HRS
DIFFICULTY: INTERMEDIATE

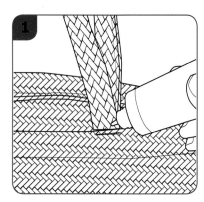

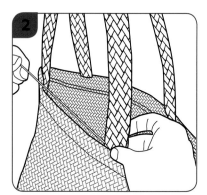

INSTRUCTIONS

1 Begin by applying fabric glue to a 1¼ inch (3 cm) length of one of the basket handles; both at the front and back, and along the sides.

2 Measure and cut a 20-inch (51-cm) length of yarn. Press one end into the glue at the back of the handle with one hand, while holding the longer end in the other hand.

HACK HINT: The discontinued **NIPPRIG** beach bag was used here, but any similar wicker basket with handles can be used.

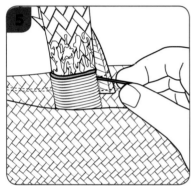

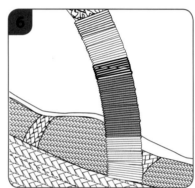

3 Swap hands and pull the longer end of the yarn around the front of the handle and across it so that the yarn sits flush to the handle and adheres with the glue.

4 Swap hands again and pull the yarn around the back then swap hands again and pull it around the front. Continue on in this rhythm, making sure that the yarn secures to the handle, until you finish wrapping your first length of yarn. You can press the yarn gently against the handle every so often to make sure it is attaching securely.

5 Secure the end of the yarn at the back of the handle with glue. Apply more fabric glue to the handle then move on to your next color, wrapping and securing the yarn in the same way.

6 Continue on around both handles, changing colors as and when you like. The stripes shown here are uneven, but you could make them all the same width.

HACK HINT: Be sure to lay out all the yarn colors before you begin to wrap the basket handles, to ensure you are happy with your chosen combination.

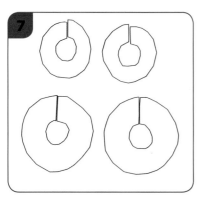

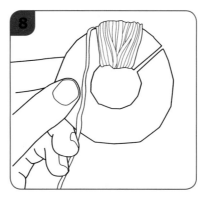

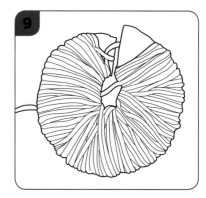

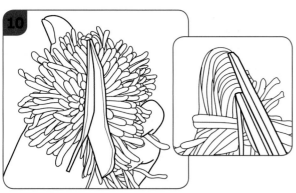

7 To make the smaller pom-pom, cut two circular pieces of card stock measuring 2¾ inches (7 cm) in diameter. Cut a 1¼-inch (3-cm) hole in the middle and then cut from the top edge into the middle of each to create a gap. For the larger pom-pom, make your circle 3½ inches (9 cm) in diameter and repeat as for the small pom-pom.

8 Starting with your smaller pom-pom, place both your cut circles together and begin to wrap your chosen yarn around the card circle, threading the yarn through the hole in the middle.

9 Keep wrapping until you have a thick, even layer of yarn all around the cut circle.

10 Next, take your scissors and cut around the pom-pom in between your two circles. Be sure to hold the pom-pom securely with your other hand to stop it from falling apart.

11 Finally cut a 24-inch (61-cm) length of yarn, double it, and place around your pom-pom in between the two card stock circles. Once you have secured your pom-pom around the middle, you can remove the card. Be sure to tie two or three knots to completely secure your pom-pom. Repeat to make the rest of your pom-poms. Tie the pom-poms to one of the handles.

PICNIC THROW

Designed by: Charlotte Rivers

Take a simple cream **GURLI** throw and add some pops of color with funky multi-hued tassels. This throw would be ideal for brightening up your summer picnic in the park.

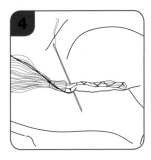

MATERIALS

IKEA® HOME FURNISHINGS **GURLI** THROW
WHITE/BEIGE, $12.99

- **28 COLORED TASSELS**
- **TAPE MEASURE OR RULER**
- **PINS**
- **NEEDLE AND THREAD**

TIME: 2 HRS
DIFFICULTY: INTERMEDIATE

INSTRUCTIONS

1 Lay your throw out on a flat surface and position your tassels around the edges. To evenly spread your tassels around the throw, leave an 8¾-inch (22-cm) gap between each tassel along the short sides and 9-inch (23-cm) gaps along the long sides. Alternate the colors as you go.

2 Pin each tassel in place around the edge of the throw.

3 Now you are ready to sew each tassel to the throw. Place a tassel flush to the edge with the loop sitting to the back of the throw. Insert at least six stitches into the base of each tassel to securely attach them to the throw.

4 Once the base is secure on the edge of the throw, you can sew the loop neatly to the back of the throw. Repeat for all 28 tassels.

FLOWER POTS

Designed by: Charlotte Rivers

This is a great way to transform a simple terracotta plant pot, before using it to pot your plant. Its small size is ideal for brightening up a window ledge, or it can be used as a centerpiece for an outdoor dining table.

MATERIALS

IKEA® HOME FURNISHINGS
INGEFÄRA FLOWER POT
AND SAUCER
TERRACOTTA, $1.99

- **ELECTRICAL TAPE**
- **X-ACTO KNIFE**
- **WHITE SPRAY PAINT**

TIME: 1 HR
DIFFICULTY: INTERMEDIATE

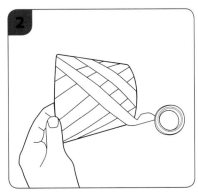

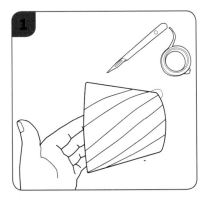

VARIATION

As an alternative to diamonds, why not try a simple striped pattern? Simply add your tape in equally spaced stripes, spray as before, and remove the tape when completely dry. You could even add a striped saucer, too.

INSTRUCTIONS

1 Begin by cutting strips of tape with an X-Acto knife and lay them down on your plant pot at a slight angle, about 1 inch (2.5 cm) apart, one after the other. As the pot is tapered, the tape will sit closer together at the bottom than it does at the top, leaving a smaller gap of approximately ⅝ inch (1.5 cm) between each piece.

2 Once you have finished laying tape in one direction, begin laying a second round of tape over the first in the other direction to create diamond shapes within the gaps. You may find it is necessary to adjust the tape, depending on the gaps created, to get the desired pattern.

3 Finally, tape around the top rim of the pot to protect it when you spray it.

4 Lay down newspaper to prepare an area outdoors for spray-painting. Take your white spray paint and spray evenly all around the pot, then allow the pot to dry for approximately 1 hour.

5 Once the pot is completely dry, carefully remove the tape. Start with the tape on the rim, then remove the top layer of tape, and finally remove the bottom layer.

STORAGE SOLUTIONS

WHO DOESN'T NEED MORE STORAGE SPACE? WE
NEVER SEEM TO HAVE ENOUGH, DESPITE ALL OUR
BEST INTENTIONS. THE PROJECTS IN THIS CHAPTER
WILL INSPIRE YOU TO TURN USEFUL HOUSEHOLD
ITEMS INTO HANDY STORAGE SPACES, LEAVING YOU
WITH MORE ROOM—AND A TIDIER HOME.

PLANTER BOXES

Designed by: Jane Hughes

These fabulous planters are an ideal size for windowsills. The plants give the faces some "hair," so you can have some fun choosing which ones to put in—herbs are ideal. The cork legs leave space for air to circulate underneath to keep your plants healthy.

MATERIALS

IKEA® HOME FURNISHINGS **FÖRHÖJA** BOX SET, $22.99

- **PENCIL**
- **PAINT: SKIN COLORS, BLACK, PINK, RED, AND BLUE**
- **PAINTBRUSHES: THICK AND THIN**
- **12 PLASTIC-TOPPED CORKS**
- **CLEAR VARNISH SPRAY**
- **STRONG GLUE**
- **4 EMPTY PLASTIC MILK CARTONS, OR SIMILAR**

TIME: 6–8 HRS
DIFFICULTY: BASIC

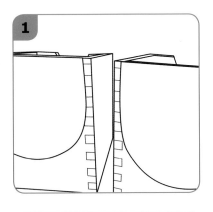

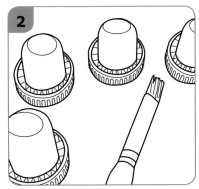

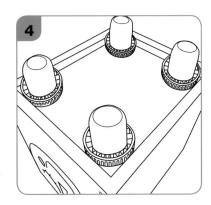

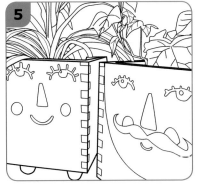

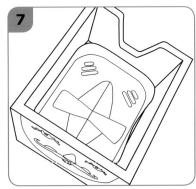

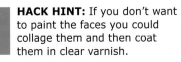

HACK HINT: If you don't want to paint the faces you could collage them and then coat them in clear varnish.

INSTRUCTIONS

1 The **FÖRHÖJA** box set has four pieces: two small boxes, one large box, and a lid/tray. The lid/tray is not required for this project so place it aside. Turn the boxes so the notch is at the back on the two smaller-sized ones. Lightly sketch the shape of a face onto the upper part of each wooden box. Paint the face shape with skin-color paint and allow it to dry.

2 Paint the corks in a bright color and allow them to dry.

3 Once the corks are dry, lay down newspaper outdoors, and spray a coat of clear varnish over them to seal in the color.

4 When the varnish is dry, glue the corks to the underside of the box in each corner.

5 Lightly pencil in the facial features and use a fine brush to paint them on neatly.

6 Once dry, spray the faces with clear varnish to seal in the colors and waterproof the paint.

7 Take four plastic milk cartons, or similar, and cut them down to 2¼ inches (6 cm) high. Place one in each of the small planter boxes and two in the large planter box to protect them from water damage.

STORAGE BASKETS

Designed by: Charlotte Rivers

This project takes a set of three small bathroom storage baskets and adds a "color-dipped" effect to them. Pastel shades have been used here, but you could select three different complementary colors of your choice.

MATERIALS

IKEA® HOME FURNISHINGS **LJUSNAN** BASKETS SEAGRASS, $5.99, SET OF 3

- **TAPE MEASURE**
- **3 PAINT COLORS: SLATE GRAY, DUCK EGG BLUE, AND CORAL**
- **PAINTBRUSH**

TIME: 1 HR
DIFFICULTY: BASIC

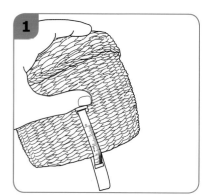

INSTRUCTIONS

1 Once you have decided on your three colors, choose the depth of paint that you would like on each basket, using a tape measure against the sides. Here, ⅝ inch (1.5 cm) is used for the smaller basket, ¾ inch (2 cm) is used for the middle basket, and 1¼ inch (3 cm) is used for the larger basket.

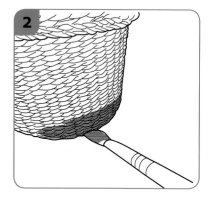

2 You can now begin to paint each basket. It is not necessary to mark the paint level with tape, as you can simply follow the groove of the basket weave at the level you wish to paint at.

3 Once all the baskets are painted, leave them to dry for approximately 20 minutes and then apply a second coat of paint to each basket.

JEWELRY BOX

Designed by: Charlotte Rivers

This hack transforms a set of **MOPPE** office storage drawers into a pretty jewelry box. The smaller set of drawers is used here, but there is a larger set that could also be used for extra storage.

HACK HINT: Take the screws that come with the **FÅGLAVIK** handles to your local hardware store and ask them to cut them in half, as they are too long for the drawers.

MATERIALS

IKEA® HOME FURNISHINGS **MOPPE** MINI CHEST OF DRAWERS BIRCH PLYWOOD, $14.99

IKEA® HOME FURNISHINGS **FÅGLAVIK** KNOBS ANY COLOR, $4.99/2 PACK

- **PLAIN FABRIC: 30 X 8¼ INCHES (76 X 21 CM)**
- **2 PIECES OF PLAIN FABRIC: 10¾ X ¾ INCHES (27 X 2 CM)**
- **4 PIECES OF PATTERNED FABRIC: 19 X 4¾ INCHES (48 X 12 CM)**
- **SCISSORS**
- **FABRIC GLUE**
- **SPATULA**
- **TAPE MEASURE**
- **PENCIL**
- **POWER DRILL AND ⁵/₃₂-INCH (4-MM) DRILL BIT**

TIME: 2–3 HRS
DIFFICULTY: INTERMEDIATE

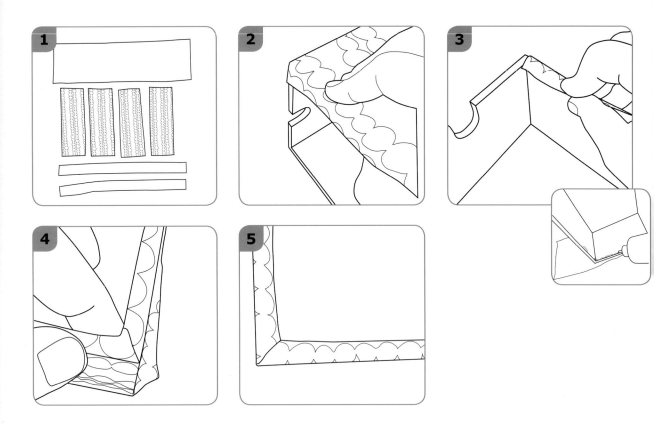

INSTRUCTIONS

1 Begin by cutting out your fabric, following the measurements given on page 65. Contrasting fabrics have been used here: a plain fabric for the drawer housing and a patterned fabric for the drawers.

2 Take one of the drawers and turn it around so that the front becomes the back, i.e., the half circle handle will be at the back. You will only be covering three sides of each drawer; the back (with the semicircle handle) will remain uncovered. Apply fabric glue to the outside of the drawer, as well as the top and bottom rims. Use a spatula to ensure that the glue is spread smoothly and evenly. You can then apply your first piece of fabric.

3 Take a piece of the patterned fabric, and rub it on smoothly with your hands to avoid any bumps. Turn it over and press carefully along the edges at the top and the bottom for a neat finish. Continue around the sides of your drawer, applying glue and then securing the fabric as you go.

4 To ensure you have neat corners, fold and secure well with extra glue (if necessary). The top corners of the drawers should look as shown in the diagram.

5 The bottom corners of the drawers should look as shown in the diagram.

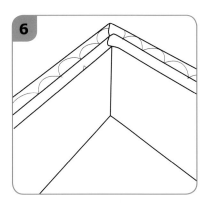

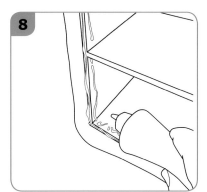

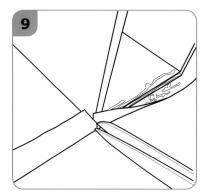

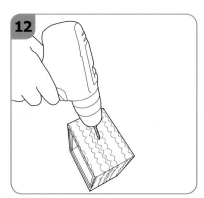

6 The inside of each drawer should look as shown in the diagram.

7 Repeat Steps 2–6 for each of your drawers.

8 Now cover the drawer housing with the plain fabric. Begin by applying fabric glue all around the outer sides of the drawer housing using a spatula to spread the glue evenly, and apply the larger piece of plain fabric. Run a little glue along the edges and inside of the housing, and fold the fabric over neatly to the inside.

9 Make small cuts in the fabric at the middle and the bottom shelves, to prevent the fabric from bunching up in the corners.

10 Once the outer fabric is on, you can then apply the final two smaller strips of plain fabric across the middle shelf and the bottom shelf. Allow the drawers and the drawer housing to dry overnight.

11 You are now ready to secure the knobs to the drawers. Measure in 2½ inches (6.5 cm) and up 2 inches (5 cm) and mark a dot on each drawer.

12 Take your drill and use a ⁵/₃₂-inch (4-mm) drill bit to drill a hole into the marked spot on each of your drawers. Now you can secure the knobs to the drawers. Allow the jewelry box to dry completely overnight before putting the drawers back into the drawer housing.

COPPER SHELVING

Designed by: Jessica Mayhall

Dress up the all-white **EKBY ALEX/EKBY LERBERG** shelf unit. Metal leaf is a quick and easy way to add style to the basic shelf unit.

MATERIALS

IKEA® HOME FURNISHINGS **EKBY ALEX/ EKBY LERBERG** SHELF WITH DRAWER WHITE, $50.99

- **PAINTBRUSH**
- **NATURAL BRISTLE BRUSH**
- **GILDING SIZE**
- **COPPER LEAF SHEETS**
- **COPPER KNOBS (OPTIONAL)**

TIME: 2 HRS
DIFFICULTY: INTERMEDIATE

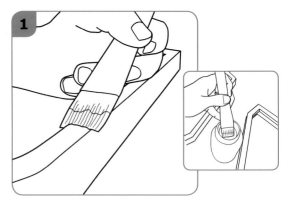

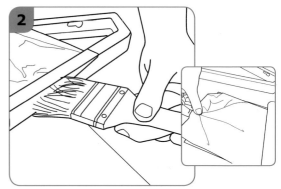

INSTRUCTIONS

1 Use a paintbrush to apply gilding size to the metal brackets. Allow it to dry.

2 Once dry, apply copper leaf sheets to the metal brackets and tamp down with a natural bristle brush. The dry size will "catch" the thin metal sheets. Continue this process until the metal brackets are completely covered with copper leaf.

3 Hang the shelving unit on the wall, following the assembly instructions.

4 Add coordinating copper knobs to the drawers, if desired.

OUTDOOR STORAGE

Designed by: Jessica Mayhall

The hardworking, durable **ÄPPLARÖ** outdoor storage bench has been given a bright, fun makeover, painted with a colorful ombré effect. It now houses toys rather than garden hoses!

MATERIALS

IKEA® HOME FURNISHINGS **ÄPPLARÖ**
STORAGE BENCH, OUTDOOR
BROWN STAINED, $70.00

- **CHALK PAINT® BY ANNIE SLOAN IN BLUE AND WHITE**
- **PAINTBRUSH**

TIME: 3 HRS
DIFFICULTY: INTERMEDIATE

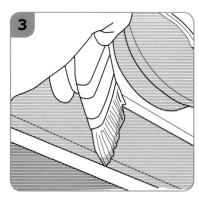

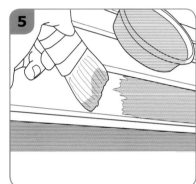
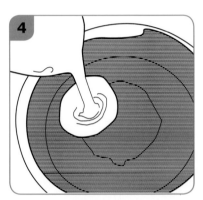
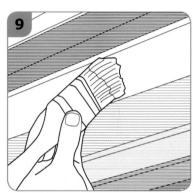

INSTRUCTIONS

1 First, assemble the storage bench following the assembly instructions. Next, apply blue paint to the outer slats, the corners on all four sides and the top piece. This will create a border in the deepest shade of color.

2 Add equal parts of white paint and blue paint together (one part blue paint to one part white) and mix thoroughly for a lightened shade of blue.

3 Use this lightened shade to paint the slat directly above the painted blue slat on all four sides and the top.

4 Add another part white paint to the lightened blue paint (now one part blue paint to two parts white). Mix thoroughly.

5 Paint the next slat on all four sides and the top with this lightened shade of blue.

6 Add one part white paint to lightened blue shade and mix thoroughly (now one part blue paint to three parts white).

7 Paint the next slat on all four sides and top with this lightened shade of blue.

8 Add one part white paint to lightened blue paint and mix thoroughly (now one part blue paint to four parts white).

9 Paint the remaining slat on all four sides and the top with this lightest shade of blue paint to finish. Leave to dry completely.

BAR CABINET

Designed by: Jessica Mayhall

In this project, the IKEA® home furnishings **PS 2014** secretary unit performs a double duty as a gorgeous bar cabinet. The plain white and natural birch finish has been updated with a fun, bright, fabric for the ultimate in entertaining.

MATERIALS

IKEA® HOME FURNISHINGS **IKEA® PS 2014** SECRETARY
WHITE/BIRCH VENEER, $189.00

- **DECOUPAGE GLUE/SEALER SUCH AS MOD PODGE**
- **FABRIC: 1 YARD (90 CM)**
- **PAINTBRUSH**
- **FLAT EDGE (E.G., SCRAPER, CREDIT CARD)**
- **SCISSORS**
- **X-ACTO KNIFE OR BOX CUTTER**

TIME: 6 HRS
DIFFICULTY: INTERMEDIATE

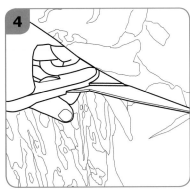

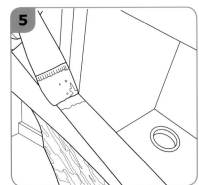

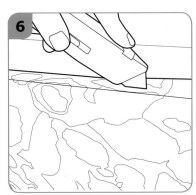

INSTRUCTIONS

1 First, assemble the unit following the assembly instructions. Apply decoupage glue/sealer to the bottom of the desktop. (This is the most visible portion of natural wood when the desk is closed.)

2 Place your fabric on the wet decoupage glue/sealer. Adjust and straighten it as necessary.

3 Apply pressure with your hands to secure the fabric to the decoupage glue/sealer. Use a flat edge, such as a scraper, to smooth out any wrinkles and to ensure a good bond between the fabric and decoupage glue/sealer. Leave to dry.

4 Trim away any excess fabric using a sharp pair of scissors.

5 Apply a generous coat of decoupage glue/sealer over the fabric to act as a sealer and allow it to dry.

6 Trim the fabric with an X-Acto knife or box cutter to get a clean edge.

7 Repeat Steps 1–6 to cover the sides and the back of the interior of the cabinet with fabric.

ORGANIZATION STATION

Designed by: Nancy Chace

Keep everyday business at bay by outfitting this deceptively spacious cabinet into a command center, ready to keep mail and devices neatly hidden away. You could also consider other drawer organization configurations, as well as wall-mount file organizers that could be attached to cabinet doors.

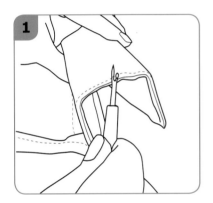

MATERIALS

IKEA® HOME FURNISHINGS **STÄLL** SHOE CABINET WITH FOUR COMPARTMENTS WHITE, $89.99

4 X IKEA® HOME FURNISHINGS **STICKAT** BED POCKETS GREEN, $4.99 EACH

- **SEAM RIPPER**
- **SCISSORS**
- **TAPE MEASURE**
- **VELCRO (HOOK AND LOOP TAPE): 2 YARDS (1.8 M)**
- **WATERCOLOR PENCIL**
- **RULER OR SET SQUARE**
- **1-INCH (2.5-CM) WIDE PAINTER'S TAPE**
- **SANDPAPER OR SANDING BLOCK: 220 GRIT**
- **TACK CLOTH**
- **NO-PRIME PAINT IN 3 COORDINATING COLORS**
- **PAINTBRUSH**
- **X-ACTO KNIFE**
- **SCRIPT LINER BRUSH**
- **SOFT FINISHING WAX, CLEAR**

TIME: 30 MINS
DIFFICULTY: INTERMEDIATE

INSTRUCTIONS

1 First, assemble the shoe cabinet following the assembly instructions. Next, prepare the bed pockets. Remove the top section of each pocket (the section that fastens around the bed rail) using a seam ripper. Pull out the metal bracket on each end of the organizer, and once removed, use scissors to cut off the excess material. Cut close to the seam above the top pockets, taking care not to cut into the seam encasing the dowel or rod. The pockets should now be 10½ inches (26.5 cm) high by 15½ inches (39.5 cm) wide.

2 Measure and cut 12 pieces of Velcro tape: four 15½-inch (39.5-cm) strips, and eight 1-inch (2.5-cm) strips.

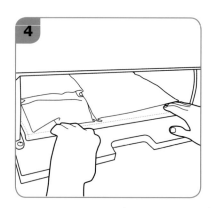

HACK HINT: To use as a charging station, thread recharging cords from outlets through the open back of the cabinet and weave the cords through the holes in the plastic drawer backs to keep them in place. Provide enough slack so the cord can reach the related device when placed in a storage pocket.

3 Affix the longer loop strip to the reverse side of the top of the fabric (the side with no pockets): peel back the self-stick tape and press firmly to secure just below the rod pocket. Attach its matching hook side to the surface, leaving the tape in place. Similarly, affix two of the 1-inch (2.5-cm) loop pieces to the lower left and right corners, attaching the matching hook pieces and leaving the tape intact. Repeat for each bed pocket.

4 Open the cabinet door and center the organizer, pocket-side-up, on the inside of the door; the longer length of Velcro tape should be closest to the drawer opening. Once you are happy with the positioning, slide the organizer down so the bottom of the fabric is close to flush with the bottom of the cabinet door. Remove the tape and press firmly to affix. Repeat for each of the cabinet doors. Close the doors.

5 Tape-off decorative stripes by measuring 3 inches (7.5 cm) from the top of the first row of drawer fronts, and lightly marking a line all the way across using a ruler and a watercolor pencil. Do the same for the sides of the cabinet, making sure the marks line up with those marked on the front. Make nine lines in total to mark off ten stripes. Every other stripe will be painted. Starting at the top of the cabinet, the first stripe will be painted, the second will not, etc.

6 Affix painter's tape in one continuous piece *below* the first 3-inch (7.5-cm) line, from left to right around all visible sides of the cabinet. Use a set square or ruler to check measurements at several points to ensure the tape line is level, and adjust as needed. Place the next row of painter's tape *above* the next line in one continuous piece. Follow this pattern until all stripes are taped off.

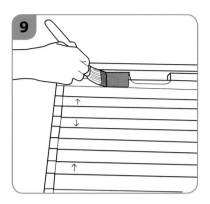

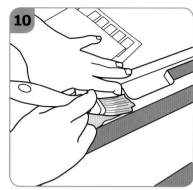

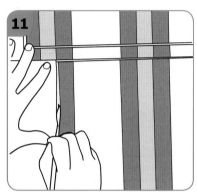

HACK HINT: Try laying the furniture on its back when taping off stripes.

7 Begin by scuff sanding only the surface to be painted—the 3-inch (7.5-cm) stripes and the bottom section or pedestal and legs— with 220 grit sandpaper and wipe clean with a tack cloth.

8 Now affix a length of painter's tape across the center of each stripe to be painted. Make sure it is level, as in Step 6.

9 Apply a no-prime paint in the colors of your choice to the masked off stripes (we have painted ours blue) and the bottom section (we have painted ours green). Let the first coat dry for 48 hours and then apply your finish coats. Remove all tape. Carefully and gently scrape any dried paint seepage with an X-Acto knife, and wipe with a tack cloth.

10 Similarly, paint the 1-inch (2.5-cm) center stripe in a coordinating color (example is green). Clean up any mistakes as you go with a damp paper towel or cotton swab. Leave to dry.

11 Using a liner brush and ruler as a guide, paint lines on either side of the 1-inch (2.5-cm) stripe (example is pink). Use a damp brush or thin the paint slightly with water to get better flow. Clean up any paint seepage as you go with a cotton swab. Recoat as needed. Don't worry if the lines aren't perfect, it will give the piece a painterly effect.

12 Once the last coat of paint is dry, seal the painted surfaces only with a soft, clear finishing wax.

ROLLING BAR CART

Designed by: Elyse Major

MATERIALS

IKEA® HOME FURNISHINGS **HEMNES** NIGHTSTAND WHITE, $69.99

- **TAPE MEASURE**
- **ROTARY SAW (OR HAND SAW)**
- **½-INCH (1.2-CM) PLYWOOD: 12 X 14⅝ INCHES (30.5 X 37 CM)**
- **SANDPAPER: MEDIUM GRIT**
- **PENCIL**
- **RULER**
- **POWER DRILL**
- **4 CONSTRUCTION SCREWS: #6, 1½ INCHES (4 CM) LONG**
- **4 LIGHT DUTY SWIVEL BEARING CASTERS: 1⅝ INCHES (4 CM) AND MOUNTING SCREWS**
- **SCREWDRIVERS**
- **COPING SAW**
- **½-INCH (1.2-CM) DECORATIVE WOOD MOLDING: 2 STRIPS MEASURING 48 INCHES (122 CM); 1 STRIP MEASURING 24 INCHES (61 CM)**
- **HAMMER**
- **8 WIRE BRADS: #18, ⅝ INCH (1.5 CM) LONG**
- **PATIO DOOR HANDLE**
- **2 HOOKS: SMALL SINGLE PRONG**
- **MOUNTABLE BOTTLE OPENER**
- **PAINTER'S TAPE**
- **METALLIC SPRAY PAINT**
- **DECORATIVE PAPER, METALLIC EMBOSSED SHOWN**
- **CRAFT GLUE**
- **GLUE STICK**
- **RHINESTONE TRIM**
- **SMALL PIECE OF CRAFTER'S ALUMINUM SHEET: 1 X 3 INCHES (2.5 X 7.5 CM)**
- **SCISSORS**

TIME: 1½ HRS+
DIFFICULTY: ADVANCED

Outfit this nightstand into a bar cart, ready to stock with your favorite drinks. You can roll the party from room to room!

INSTRUCTIONS

1 Assemble the nightstand following the assembly instructions. Then, using a tape measure, measure the bottom perimeter of the cart defined by the legs. Use a rotary saw to cut a piece of plywood to serve as a base of the same size. In this example, this base was 12 inches (30.5 cm) by 14⅝ inches (37 cm), although yours may vary slightly. Sand all the edges until smooth.

2 Place the cart on top of the plywood base so that each leg fits into a corner of the base. In pencil, lightly mark the top and front of the base for future reference. The top is the side that faces the underside of the included shelf; the front is the edge on the same side as the table's drawer pull.

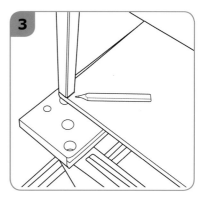

3 Use a pencil to trace each leg's footprint onto the base. Use a ruler and pencil to find the center of the traced areas.

4 Drill pilot holes through the center points using a bit suitable for a #6 1½-inch (4-cm) construction screw.

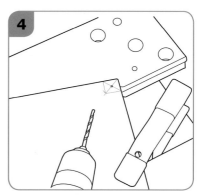

5 Turn the table over onto the floor. Be sure to place it on a surface that won't scratch its top. Place the plywood base on the legs of the table, aligning the top and front accordingly.

6 Drill through the holes you made in the plywood base so that the pilot holes are extended into each leg of the table. Affix the plywood base to the legs of the table with construction screws. Place a caster in one corner of the plywood base and use a pencil to mark points for the mounting screws. Do this for each corner of the plywood base. Drill pilot holes where indicated by your pencil marks. The holes should be drilled with a bit appropriate for the size of the mounting screws. (Be sure not to have the casters in place when drilling the pilot holes.)

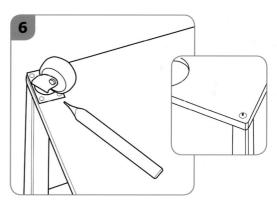

7 Working one corner at a time, position each caster over its pilot hole and install to the bottom of the plywood base using a screwdriver and the included screws. Be sure all casters are installed to face the same direction.

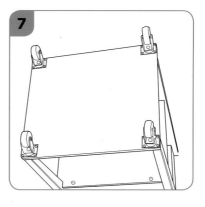

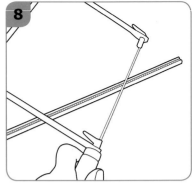

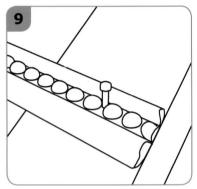

8 Use the coping saw to cut the decorative molding into four 15-inch (38-cm) strips and four 11⅞-inch (30-cm) strips. The first 48-inch (122 cm) strip will yield three 15-inch (38 cm) pieces, the second 48-inch (122 cm) will yield one 15-inch (38-cm) piece and two 11⅞-inch (30-cm) pieces, and the 24-inch (61-cm) strip will yield the remaining two 11⅞-inch (30-cm) pieces. Lightly sand all the cut ends until smooth.

9 Turn the unit on its right side and install one 11⅞-inch (30-cm) strip to the left side legs, 4 inches (10 cm) above the plywood base hammering in place with the wire brads. Install another 11⅞-inch (30-cm) piece 4 inches (10 cm) above the included upper shelf. These strips should be flush with the edge of each leg. Turn the unit on its left side and affix two more 11⅞-inch (30-cm) strips to the right side as before.

10 Positioning the unit as needed, install the 15-inch (38-cm) strips to the front and back, 4 inches (10 cm) above each shelf. Each strip should extend beyond the edge of the table legs and cover the ends of the molding strips added to each side.

11 Turn the unit upside down, placing it on a sturdy surface that won't scratch the top. Place the patio door handle on the table's left side, under the tabletop. Center it and then drill pilot holes for the mounting screws, being very careful not to drill all the way through the top.

12 Install the handle to the top using the included hardware.

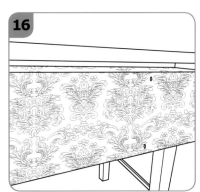

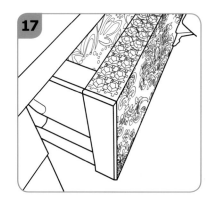

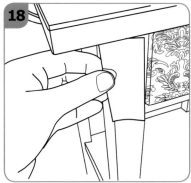

13 Turn the unit right side up and attach the two hooks to the right side legs, about 4 inches (10 cm) from the top.

14 Remove the included drawer pull and replace with a bottle opener, mounting it with its included hardware. Remove the opener and screws prior to painting and adding decorative paper (see Step 19).

15 Lay down newspaper to prepare an area outdoors for spray-painting. Cover the top with painter's tape so it remains unpainted, then spray-paint the unit silver. Leave to dry, and then repeat to add as many coats as desired. Allow it to dry well before removing the tape.

16 Measure and cut decorative paper to size in order to line the inside of the drawer and the drawer front. Affix using the glue stick and craft glue.

17 Add a length of rhinestone trim to decorate the inner top edge of the drawer, if desired.

18 Glue the small piece of aluminum metal in place at the front of the bar cart, alongside the drawer, to allow for holding any small bar tools or caps with magnets.

19 Using the fine point of a pair of scissors, gently poke holes through the paper to reinstall the bottle opener.

OCCASIONAL TABLE

Designed by: Danielle Driscoll

Structural additions, shimmering hardware, and decorative paint effects take this hardworking piece from streamline to coastline. Any occasional table with drawers can be used.

> **HACK HINT:** The discontinued **NORDEN** occasional table was used here, but any similar unit with three drawers can be used.

MATERIALS

OCCASIONAL TABLE WITH THREE DRAWERS

- **1 x 6 INCH (2.5 x 15 CM) COMMON BOARD: 8 FOOT (240 CM) LONG**
- **TABLE SAW**
- **MITER SAW**
- **POWER DRILL**
- **SANDPAPER, MEDIUM GRIT**
- **CHALK PAINT® BY ANNIE SLOAN IN FRENCH LINEN, PURE WHITE, GRAPHITE, AND LOUIS BLUE**
- **PLASTIC CUP AND WATER**
- **PAINTBRUSHES: FLAT AND ROUND BRISTLE**
- **WATER IN SPRAY BOTTLE AND TEXTURED PAPER TOWEL**
- **SOFT FINISHING WAX, CLEAR**
- **WAXING BRUSH**
- **CHEESE CLOTH**
- **MERCURY GLASS KNOBS**

TIME: 1 HR+
DIFFICULTY: ADVANCED

INSTRUCTIONS

1 Begin to assemble the table following the assembly instructions. When you reach the drawer assembly, cut new drawer fronts from the common board to replace the original ones. First, run the board through a table saw to match the drawer front height—about 5¼ inches (13 cm). Lower the table saw blade to the depth of the groove in the original drawer front, then move the saw guide so that it is in the same position. Cut the groove along the full length of the board. Cut three pieces from the prepared board to the width of the original drawer fronts using a miter saw.

2 Drill holes in the back of your new drawer fronts, matching the depth and position of the originals. Drill holes for hardware at center front. Complete the table assembly.

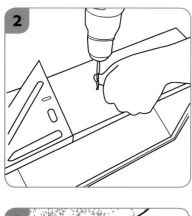

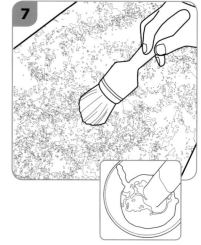

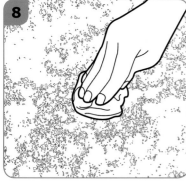

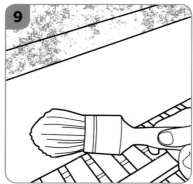

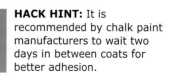

HACK HINT: It is recommended by chalk paint manufacturers to wait two days in between coats for better adhesion.

3 Scuff-sand the table including the new drawer fronts, to give the wood "tooth" to enable the paint to cling to it.

4 Pour French Linen chalk paint into a plastic cup, add some water, and stir. For a hint of color over the wood grain, apply the watered-down paint as a wash, using a flat brush and long, even strokes.

5 For a driftwood finish, apply a Pure White wash over the French Linen, as before.

6 To give the top a soapstone appearance, first apply undiluted Graphite chalk paint, using a textured brush in hashed strokes. Allow the paint to dry and add a second coat.

7 Next, mix Louis Blue chalk paint with water, and paint onto the surface with a flat brush.

8 Immediately spritz with water and blot with a textured paper towel. For best results, work in small sections, as the paint is quick to dry. If an area begins to dry before you've finished the effect, simply spritz more water over it.

9 Seal your faux finish with soft, clear finishing wax; using a wax brush, apply a small amount and wipe off any excess with cheese cloth. Wait 24 hours for additional coats of wax. For the project shown, two coats of wax were applied all over, with three coats to the top. Complete by adding the knobs to the drawer fronts.

PANTRY CUPBOARD

Designed by: Elyse Major

The tall height and small footprint of this bookcase make it perfect for pantry storage. The addition of a fabric-backed, chicken wire screen door gives the piece a shabby chic appeal, while keeping your groceries hidden away.

MATERIALS

IKEA® HOME FURNISHINGS **BILLY** BOOKCASE BIRCH VENEER, $69.99

- ½ X 1½ INCH (1.2 X 4 CM) MAPLE: 4 PIECES MEASURING 48 INCHES (122 CM); 1 PIECE MEASURING 24 INCHES (61 CM)
- COMPOUND MITER SAW OR MITER BOX WITH SAW
- 4 FLAT CORNER BRACES WITH SCREWS, SMALL: 1½–2 INCHES (4–5 CM)
- POWER DRILL WITH ASSORTED DRILL BITS
- 2 T-PLATES: 3 INCHES (7.5 CM), WITH SCREWS
- PENCIL
- WORK GLOVES
- CHICKEN WIRE: CUT TO 76 X 15½ INCHES (193 X 39.5 CM)
- STAPLE GUN
- ¼-INCH (5-MM) STAPLE GUN STAPLES
- CRAFT GLUE
- RESIN APPLIQUÉS
- WHITE PRIMER SPRAY
- PAINT
- FOAM OR FLAT PAINTBRUSH
- 3 BROAD HINGES: 2 X 1³⁄₈ INCHES (5 X 3.5 CM), WITH SCREWS
- SCREWDRIVERS
- CABINET MAGNET WITH SCREWS
- HACKSAW
- KNOB WITH MOUNTING SCREW
- FABRIC: 1 YARD (90 CM)
- TACKS

TIME: 1 HR
DIFFICULTY: ADVANCED

HACK HINT: Due to the height of the cupboard door frame, you may need to use more than a single piece of fabric to create the decorative cloth panel. For a seamless look, aim to stitch or fuse fabric together where the horizontal wood section covers it.

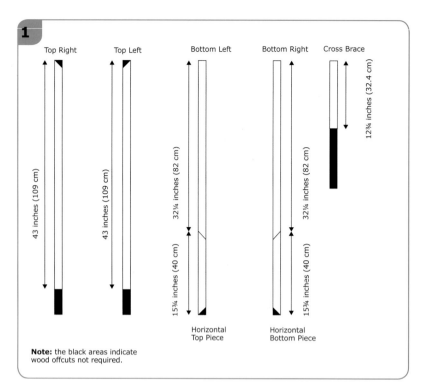

Note: the black areas indicate wood offcuts not required.

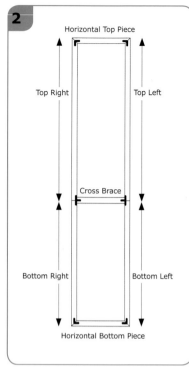

INSTRUCTIONS

1 Using a miter saw, cut the seven pieces of wood you require to make the door following the cutting guide shown in the diagram above and cutting the wood at a 45-degree angle where shown.

2 Arrange the pieces following the placement diagram above right, remembering that you are placing the pieces with their back side up (and therefore right and left will be reversed until you turn the finished door over). Attach the corner braces to each corner (following the manufacturer's instructions and drilling pilot holes if needed). Attach the T-plates to fix the cross brace in place, as shown on the diagram.

3 Turn the assembled door over and drill a hole for the knob, centered horizontally on the right side, 4–6 inches (10–15 cm) above the cross brace.

4 Hold the newly-constructed door to the **BILLY** bookcase and determine where you would like to place the three hinges. There should be one near the top, one near the bottom, and one near the center. Placement will depend upon the position of the adjustable shelves. Use a pencil to mark the position of the hinges on the back of the door by tracing the shape of the hinge.

5 Place the door front face down on a sturdy work surface. Position the chicken wire on the back of the door, centering it as best you can.

HACK HINT: Take care when working with chicken wire by wearing work gloves to protect your fingers; the wire ends will be especially sharp after they have been snipped.

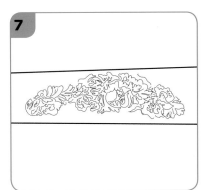

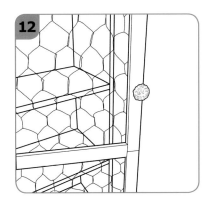

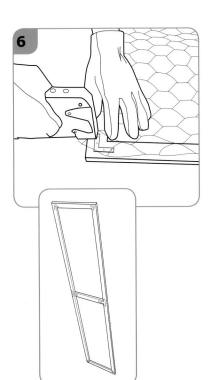

HACK HINT: Use the concept of fashioning a door for the **BILLY** and make it your own. You could, for example, affix a series of narrow shutters applying the hinge technique explained here, or suspend a small dowel and hang a curtain or beads.

6 Use the staple gun to attach the chicken wire to the back of the door. When stapling, be aware of your pencil marks indicating the placement of the hinges and avoid stapling inside the traced area.

7 Use glue to affix any decorative appliqués to the door frame front. Apply an overall coat of white primer to the door only and leave to dry.

8 When the paint is dry, attach the hinges to the back of the door in the areas you traced in pencil (see Step 4).

9 Place the **BILLY** bookcase on the floor on its back. Put the door in place then lift it, as if you were opening it on the hinges, to see where you should attach the hinges on the bookcase. You may need a helper to hold the door while you attach the other half of each hinge to the bookcase.

10 Attach the cabinet magnet to the bookcase near the cross brace, so that the magnet catches on the T-plate when the door is closed.

11 Brush on a light and imperfect coat or two of paint to the entire exterior of the bookcase, avoiding the chicken wire on the door. If using chalk paint be sure to follow with soft, clear finishing wax as recommended.

12 Attach the knob to the door through the hole previously drilled. Use a hacksaw to cut the knob's screw to its nut.

13 Stand the cabinet back up and attach the cloth backing to the back of the door, using tacks to keep it changeable (see Hack Hint on page 85).

READING BENCH

Designed by: Charlotte Rivers

Turning the **KALLAX** shelving unit on its side and adding a
comfortable padded seat creates a great little reading bench,
which still has storage for books and toys underneath. If you had
a corner spot, you could even make two to create L-shaped seating.

MATERIALS

IKEA® HOME FURNISHINGS
KALLAX SHELVING UNIT
WITH FOUR COMPARTMENTS
BIRCH EFFECT, $59.99

- **MEDIUM-DENSITY
  FIBERBOARD (MDF):
  15½ X 57½ INCHES
  (39.5 X 146 CM)**
- **1-INCH (2.5-CM) HIGH-
  DENSITY UPHOLSTERY
  FOAM: 15½ X 57½ INCHES
  (39.5 X 146 CM)**
- **FABRIC: 29½ X 71 INCHES
  (75 X 180 CM)**
- **SCISSORS**
- **STAPLE GUN AND STAPLES**
- **6 2-INCH (5-CM) SCREWS**
- **POWER DRILL**

TIME: 2–3 HRS
DIFFICULTY: ADVANCED

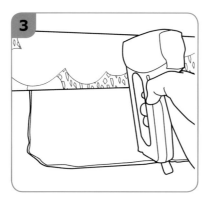

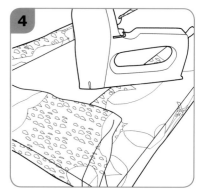

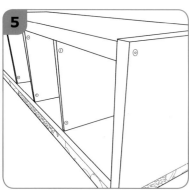

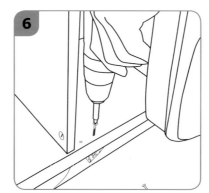

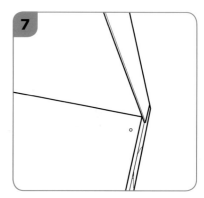

INSTRUCTIONS

1 Begin by assembling the **KALLAX** shelving unit following the assembly instructions. Turn the assembled unit on its side.

2 Next, lay your MDF board out on a flat surface. Place the foam on top of the board and the fabric on top of the foam. Position the fabric so it is centered over the foam.

3 Carefully turn the MDF board/foam/fabric sandwich over. Now, begin to pull the fabric around to the back of the MDF and secure it using a staple gun. Go slowly, checking you are pulling the fabric taut to avoid wrinkles.

4 At the corners, fold the fabric in neatly, as if wrapping a present, then staple in place.

5 Once all the fabric is secured, lay the seat pad face down on the floor (ensuring that the floor is clean) and place the **KALLAX** shelving unit on top. Be sure to line up the shelves with the seat pad.

6 You will see that there are a number of existing holes down one side of the shelving unit. You can use these holes to secure one side of your seat pad to the shelves using a drill and three 2-inch (5 cm) screws.

7 When it comes to securing the other side, you will need to drill yourself three holes down this side and then screw in the remaining three 2-inch (5 cm) screws. Your reading bench is now ready to use.

NIGHTSTAND

Designed by: Sarah M. Dorsey Designs

Discover how to take a simple fabric **SKUBB** drawer and transform it into a striking nightstand for your bedroom. Perfect for holding your lamp and bedtime reading in style!

MATERIALS

IKEA® HOME FURNISHINGS **SKUBB** BOX
WITH COMPARTMENTS
VARIOUS COLORS, $7.99

- **MEDIUM-DENSITY FIBERBOARD (MDF): 2 PIECES MEASURING 18½ X 14¼ INCHES (47 X 36 CM) FOR THE TOP AND BOTTOM; 2 PIECES MEASURING 14¼ X 4½ INCHES (36 X 11.5 CM) FOR THE SIDES; 1 PIECE MEASURING 17 X 5 INCHES (43 X 12.5 CM) FOR THE BACK**
- **PRIMER**
- **PAINT**
- **FLAT PAINTBRUSH**
- **GORILLA GLUE**
- **4 LARGE BAMBOO POLES: 20½ INCHES (52 CM) LONG**
- **2 X 2 INCH (5 X 5 CM) SCRAP WOOD: 6 INCHES (15 CM) LONG**
- **JIGSAW**
- **4 DOWELS: 3 INCHES (7.5 CM) LONG**
- **2 SMALL BAMBOO POLES: 20 INCHES (51 CM) LONG**
- **POWER DRILL**
- **SANDPAPER**
- **4 MOLDING LENGTHS: 14 INCHES (35.5 CM) LONG, CUT AT 45-DEGREE ANGLE**
- **WOOD FILLER**
- **⅛ INCH (3 MM) PLYWOOD: 17 X 5 INCHES (43 X 12.5 CM) FOR DRAWER FRONT**
- **FABRIC: 20 X 20 INCHES (51 X 51 CM)**
- **LONG NEEDLE AND UPHOLSTERY THREAD**

TIME: 1–2 HRS
DIFFICULTY: ADVANCED

INSTRUCTIONS

1 Begin by making an MDF box to house your fabric **SKUBB** drawer; this will form the top of the nightstand. Start by priming and painting the MDF pieces on one side only (the side that will form the inside of the box), as it is easier to do this before construction. Apply two coats of each, and allow to dry in between. (The outside of the box will be painted in Step 9.)

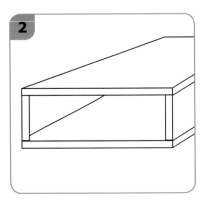

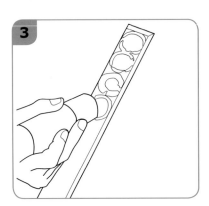

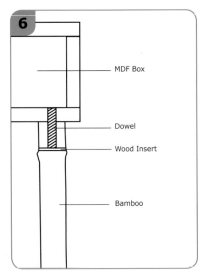

MDF Box

Dowel

Wood Insert

Bamboo

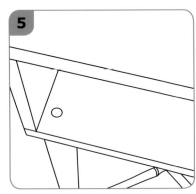

2 Next, construct your MDF box, making sure that the painted sides are placed to the inside. Take your bottom piece and glue the two side pieces in place. Then slot the back piece in between the two side pieces at the back, and glue into place. Finally glue the top on. The width goes all the way across and the height goes in between the top and bottom. The side and back pieces should be glued in between the top and bottom pieces, as shown.

3 Now create the inserts that will go inside the hollow bamboo in order to secure them to the MDF box. Take the four pieces of large bamboo (that will form the legs), dip one end of each into some paint, and press onto your 2 x 2 inch (5 x 5 cm) scrap wood; this creates a guide for cutting the wood to size. Once dry, take your jigsaw and cut the wood out around the inside of the circles made by the paint-dipped bamboo poles.

4 Now drill through the four wood pieces you have created and insert a dowel into each one. Prior to inserting the dowel into the wood piece, apply some gorilla glue to the rods to ensure they will be extra secure. Then, place the insert with the dowel facing up into the top of the bamboo leg, securing it with gorilla glue.

5 Next, drill four holes (the same size as the diameter of your dowel) about 1 inch (2.5 cm) in from each corner on the underside of the MDF box you have created.

6 To secure the legs in place, apply gorilla glue to the top of each dowel and slide the dowels into the holes you drilled on the underside of your MDF box.

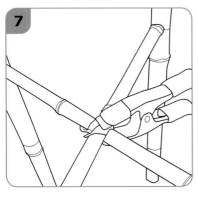

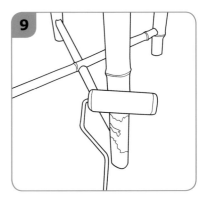

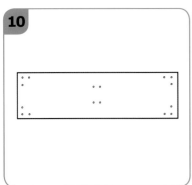

7 For the cross on the bottom, position the two small pieces of bamboo in place then measure and mark where they cross over in the middle. Drill a large hole at the point where they cross and then widen it so you can sit the top piece of the cross into the bottom. Use gorilla glue to secure the top piece in place, and then use clamps while it dries to ensure that it bonds tightly.

8 Next you can attach your molding to the top of the nightstand using gorilla glue.

9 Now you are ready to complete the painting. Begin by filling in any cracks or gaps with wood filler and allow it to dry. Sand down before applying two coats of primer and then two coats of paint. Leave to dry thoroughly between coats.

10 To make the fabric-wrapped front of your drawer, take the plywood panel and drill three holes into each corner and four in the center (for the handle).

11 Wrap the fabric around the plywood panel, glue in place at the back, then place on top of the front of the **SKUBB** drawer. Sew the panel to the drawer through the drilled holes at each corner using a long needle and upholstery thread. Ensure you sew through each section four times so it is secure.

12 Finally cut and sew a loop of fabric on the front for the handle and again attach using a needle and upholstery thread. Again, sew through four times to ensure it is secure.

STORAGE STOOL

Designed by: Audrey Smit

Taking the simple **MOLGER** storage stool and adding a colorful seat cushion is a great way of not only personalizing this useful bathroom storage box, but also turning it into a multifunctional item.

MATERIALS

IKEA® HOME FURNISHINGS
MOLGER STORAGE STOOL
BIRCH, $39.99

- **SANDPAPER**
- **PRIMER**
- **PAINT**
- **FLAT PAINTBRUSH**
- **1 SHEET OF PLYWOOD: AT LEAST 14¾ INCH (37.5 CM) SQUARE**
- **ELECTRIC SAW**
- **SCISSORS**
- **FOAM: 2 INCHES (5 CM) THICK, AT LEAST 14¾ INCH (37.5 CM) SQUARE**
- **FABRIC: 1 YARD (90 CM)**
- **STAPLE GUN AND STAPLES**
- **4 ¾-INCH (2-CM) SCREWS**
- **POWER DRILL WITH SCREWDRIVER BIT**

TIME: 3 HRS
DIFFICULTY: ADVANCED

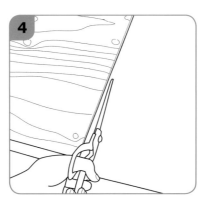

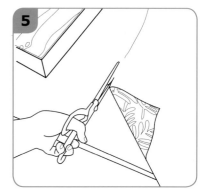

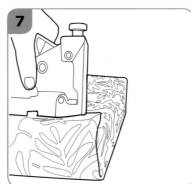

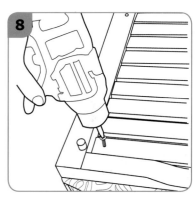

INSTRUCTIONS

1 First, assemble the storage stool following the assembly instructions.

2 Next, sand down both the stool and its detachable lid, then apply a coat of primer, followed by a coat of paint in the color of your choice. You will need to apply at least three coats of paint for good coverage. Allow each coat to dry properly in between each application.

3 Now make the cushion seat for the stool lid. Cut your plywood into a 14¾-inch (37.5-cm) square with an electric saw.

4 Then cut your foam into a 14¾-inch (37.5-cm) square to fit your plywood.

5 Cut your fabric wide enough that it will fit over the foam—top and sides—and leave an additional 1½ inches (4 cm) for stapling.

6 Stack your foam over your plywood, cover with fabric, and then turn it over; staple the fabric in place on the back of the plywood along two opposite sides of the seat.

7 Fold the fabric neatly in the corners and staple the remaining two opposite sides of your seat.

8 Lay the cushion upside down, place the lid of the stool on top, and drill a screw in at each corner to secure the seat cushion onto the lid. Place the lid onto the stool.

STYLISH SIDEBOARD

Designed by: Stephanie Jones

Turn the **KALLAX** shelving unit on its side and add plumbing pipe legs to create a unique sideboard. It would also function well as a bar, or a credenza for an office space.

MATERIALS

IKEA® HOME FURNISHINGS **KALLAX** SHELVING UNIT BIRCH EFFECT, $59.99

- **GREASE-CUTTING SOAP**
- **¾ INCH (2 CM) METAL PLUMBING PIPE SECTIONS AND CONNECTORS: 1 PIPE SECTION 48 INCHES (122 CM) LONG; 2 T-CONNECTORS; 4 PIPE SECTIONS 4 INCHES (10 CM) LONG; 4 90-DEGREE ELBOW CONNECTORS; 4 FLOOR FLANGES; 4 PIPE SECTIONS 12 INCHES (30.5 CM) LONG**
- **CHANNEL-LOCK PLIERS**
- **PENCIL**
- **POWER DRILL/SCREWDRIVER, WITH BITS AND SCREWDRIVER ATTACHMENTS**
- **QUART (1 LITER) OF ACRYLIC HIGH-BONDING PRIMER (SUCH AS THE GRIPPER BY GLIDDEN)**
- **SMALL, DENSE FOAM ROLLER AND PAINT TRAY**

- **QUART (1 LITER) OF MODERN MASTERS METALLIC PAINT IN STEEL GRAY**
- **QUART (1 LITER) OF MODERN MASTERS METAL EFFECTS PAINT IN IRON**
- **2- OR 3-INCH (5- OR 7.5-CM) SYNTHETIC-BRISTLE PAINTBRUSH**
- **2- OR 3-INCH (5- OR 7.5-CM) NATURAL-BRISTLE CHIP BRUSH**
- **16 WOOD SCREWS: #10, 1 INCH (2.5 CM) LONG**
- **16 OZ (0.5 LITER) BOTTLE MODERN MASTERS PATINA SOLUTION IN RUST**
- **SMALL SPRITZ BOTTLE**
- **SMALL DRIP BOTTLE**
- **QUART (1 LITER) OF MODERN MASTERS PERMACOAT XTREME®**

TIME: 1 DAY (PLUS AN OVERNIGHT DRY FOR THE PRIMER IF DIRECTED BY MANUFACTURER) DIFFICULTY: ADVANCED

HACK HINT: The finish on your pipework does not matter, as it will all be painted.

HACK HINT: The wet patina solution can be spattered with hydrogen peroxide and/or rubbing alcohol to intensify the rusted effect.

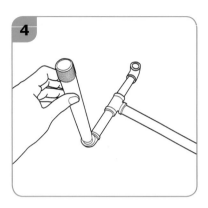

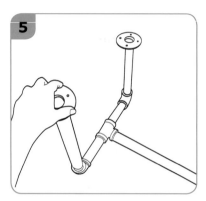

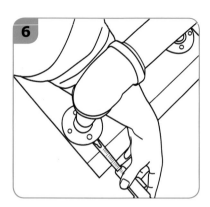

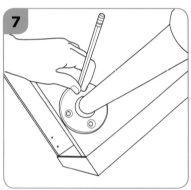

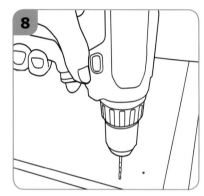

INSTRUCTIONS

1 Assemble your shelves following the assembly instructions provided.

2 With a grease-cutting soap, clean the metal plumbing pieces that will become the sideboard's legs. Allow them to dry before assembling.

3 First, take the 48-inch (122-cm) section of pipe and place a T-connector on each end, securing the pipe into the downward (middle) stems. Then secure the 4-inch (10-cm) pipes into the T-section crossbars. Secure an elbow connector to the other end of each of the 4-inch (10-cm) pipes.

4 Screw the 12-inch (30.5-cm) pipe sections into the other opening of each elbow.

5 Secure a flange to the other end of each 12-inch (30.5-cm) pipe section.

6 Use the pliers to adjust the legs level, then set them on top of the shelves, measuring to make sure they are centered.

7 Make pencil marks through the holes in the flanges, and then set the legs aside.

8 With a small drill bit, make pilot holes at each pencil mark.

9 Apply a coat of bonding primer to all surfaces, including the legs, and leave to dry overnight, or as recommended.

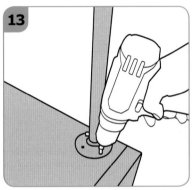

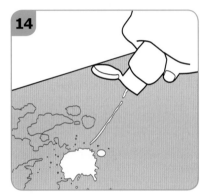

10 Using the brush or roller, apply two to three coats of the Steel Gray paint to all surfaces on the **KALLAX** shelving unit and the leg assembly, allowing the recommended drying time in between.

11 On the outer surfaces of the **KALLAX** shelving unit and on the legs, apply a coat of Iron paint and allow it to dry. Cover the surfaces well, but allow some of the Steel Gray paint to show through in places.

12 With a bristly "chip"-style brush, add a second coat of Iron paint to all the outside surfaces and legs, stippling the paint on to create texture, and again allowing spots of Steel Gray to show.

13 When the Iron paint is thoroughly dry, turn the **KALLAX** shelving unit onto its "top." Using the screws and appropriate screwdriver bit, fasten the legs to the bottom of the piece. Stand the sideboard up on its legs.

14 Pour the patina solution into the spritz and drip bottles. Apply the patina solution to the Iron paint, spraying and dripping as desired. Saturate the paint in places, but allow some areas to remain dry. Let the patina develop and dry for several hours.

15 For protection, apply Permacoat Xtreme, according to the manufacturer's instructions.

FUNCTIONAL FUN

MOST OF THE PROJECTS IN THIS CHAPTER SHOW
YOU HOW YOU CAN TURN ONE OBJECT INTO
SOMETHING COMPLETELY DIFFERENT—AND MORE
USEFUL! OFTEN REFERRED TO AS UPCYCLING, THIS
APPROACH TO HACKING WILL SAVE YOU MONEY
AND HELP YOU GET THE MOST OUT OF YOUR
BELONGINGS.

BATHROOM SHELF

Designed by: Charlotte Rivers

This project turns the classic **BEKVÄM** spice rack into a nifty little bathroom shelf, ideal for storing all your toiletries and other bathroom supplies. This is a great budget option and at the easy end of the DIY scale.

MATERIALS

IKEA® HOME FURNISHINGS **BEKVÄM** SPICE RACK BIRCH, $3.99

- **SANDPAPER**
- **GOLD SPRAY PAINT**

TIME: 2½ HRS (INCLUDING DRYING TIME)
DIFFICULTY: BASIC

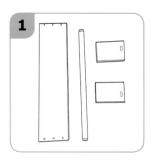

INSTRUCTIONS

1 Begin by sanding the four different pieces of wood that make up the spice rack to make them smooth to the touch. Next lay the pieces out on a flat surface. It is best to use spray paint outside, covering the area with newspaper before spraying.

2 Spray each piece of wood evenly with the gold metallic spray paint. Be sure to spray around the edges too. Once sprayed, the wood needs to be left to dry completely for approximately 1 hour.

3 Once dry, turn over each piece of wood and spray the other side. Again, leave to dry for approximately 1 hour.

4 Now you can assemble your shelf, following the assembly instructions provided.

CANDLE HOLDERS

Designed by: Elyse Major

Inexpensive clear glass candle holders are encrusted with glass glitter to add a touch of stylish sparkle wherever they are placed.

MATERIALS

IKEA® HOME FURNISHINGS
GALEJ TEALIGHT HOLDERS
CLEAR GLASS, $1.99/4 PACK

- **FOAM BRUSH**
- **DECOUPAGE GLUE/SEALER
  SUCH AS MOD PODGE**
- **GERMAN GLASS GLITTER**
- **ACRYLIC COATING SPRAY**

TIME: 30–60 MINS
DIFFICULTY: BASIC

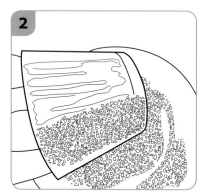

INSTRUCTIONS

1 Using a foam brush, apply a broad, even stroke of decoupage glue/sealer to the exterior of the glass candle holder.

2 Carefully pour glass glitter over the decoupage glue/sealer to cover then shake-off any excess. Allow it to set.

3 Apply your next stroke of decoupage glue/sealer, working as close to the finished strip as possible, and add glitter as before. It is easier to achieve full coverage by applying wide rows of decoupage glue/sealer rather than spreading and rolling.

4 Continue until the outside of the glass is completely covered in glitter. Fill any gaps with dabs of glue and sprinkles of glitter.

5 Apply a light application of acrylic coating spray to set the glitter. Lay newspaper down to prepare an area outdoors, and follow the manufacturer's instructions for best spraying results. Apply additional coat(s) of spray, if needed, leaving to dry in between coats, and before use.

HACK HINT: Work over a paper plate to catch excess glitter. Roll the plate into a funnel to return glitter to the bottle, checking first that there is no glue mixed in.

BOX SET DOLLHOUSE

Designed by: Jane Hughes

This dollhouse is a really versatile project. Decorate the inside in a modern, minimalist way or with total granny-chic floral. You could make it taller or wider by adding more boxes or sticking them back to back so two children can play with the house at the same time.

MATERIALS

2 X IKEA® HOME FURNISHING **HYFS** BOX SETS GRAY, $5.99/SET OF 3

- **PENCIL**
- **RULER**
- **SCISSORS**
- **CRAFT KNIFE**
- **SCRAPS OF WALLPAPER, WRAPPING PAPER, SELF-ADHESIVE VINYL, AND FELT**
- **WHITE GLUE SUCH AS ELMER'S GLUE**
- **WASHI TAPES**
- **STRONG ADHESIVE FOAM TAPE**
- **STRONG BROWN CARDBOARD**
- **BLACK MARKER**
- **DOUBLE-SIDED TAPE**
- **PAPER**
- **MAGAZINE/CATALOG PICTURES OF SMALL HOUSEHOLD ITEMS**
- **BLACK ELECTRICAL TAPE**

TIME: 6–8 HRS
DIFFICULTY: BASIC

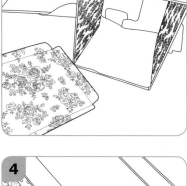

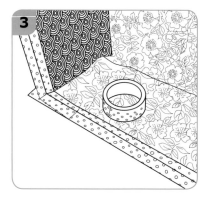

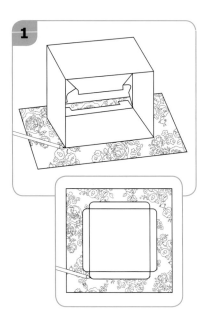

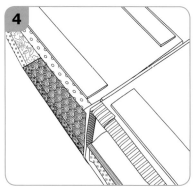

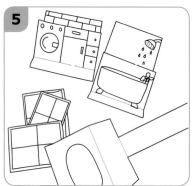

INSTRUCTIONS

1 To make this dollhouse, you will need the two larger boxes and three of the smaller boxes. Partially assemble the boxes as shown, then trace around three sides of each box and each box base onto the patterned papers for dollhouse "wallpaper."

2 Cut out the wallpaper sheets and use white glue to stick them in place onto each box base, and onto the three interior side "walls" of each box "room." (Note: the back wall of the room will be covered by the box base when the box assembly is completed in Step 3.) Trace the shape of the remaining side of each box onto felt or flooring paper, cut out the felt piece, and stick them down to make the "floor" of each room.

3 Once the glue has thoroughly dried, complete the box assembly by fitting the box base in place. Cover the open edges of the assembled boxes with washi tapes.

4 Using the adhesive foam tape, attach the boxes together.

5 To make the cardboard furniture, draw and cut out shapes for the windows, kitchen, log burner, etc. from strong brown cardboard. Draw on details with a black marker. To create a 3D look, fold the cardboard three times.

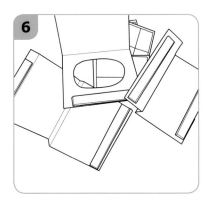

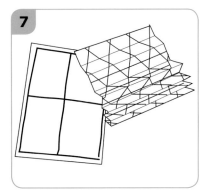

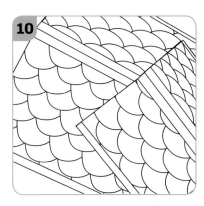

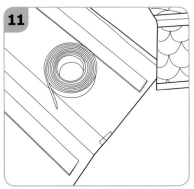

6 Using double-sided tape, stick the cardboard details onto the walls and floors.

7 Make blinds by cutting a piece of paper slightly larger than the window. Concertina fold half of the paper and attach with double-sided tape to the top of the window.

8 Cut out small pictures of household items (telephones, paintings, etc.) and stick down in each room.

9 Cut two cardboard pieces, 8¾ x 8 inches (22.5 x 20 cm) and 6¼ x 4¼ inches (16 x 11 cm). Fold in half to make roof shapes.

10 Draw on roof tiles and add the black electrical tape to the front/back edges and along the fold.

11 Add adhesive foam tape to the underside of the roof and attach in place to finish.

12 Fill the finished house with dollhouse furniture, accessories, and people.

PAINTED BLOCKS

Designed by: Stephanie Jones

Using the lightweight fabric **SKUBB** boxes as a base, this hack creates charming storage for a nursery or child's playroom. The charcoal gray and white shades work well in any color scheme.

HACK HINT: Use the lid from the paint can as your palette, to ensure that you don't overload the brush.

MATERIALS

IKEA® HOME FURNISHINGS **SKUBB** BOXES WHITE, $7.99/SET OF 6

- **SAMPLE-SIZED CANS OF CHALK PAINT® BY ANNIE SLOAN IN GRAPHITE AND OLD WHITE (OR ANOTHER FLAT-FINISH, HIGH-ADHESION PAINT IN SIMILAR COLORS)**
- **2-INCH (5-CM) NATURAL BRISTLE BRUSH**
- **LOW-TACK ADHESIVE SPRAY**
- **SMALL ALPHABET STENCILS, E.G., LETTER STENCILS BY MARTHA STEWART CRAFTS**
- **PAINTER'S TAPE**
- **SMALL ¼-INCH (5-MM) OR ½-INCH (1.2-CM) STENCILING BRUSH**
- **PAPER TOWELS**

TIME: 1–2 HRS
DIFFICULTY: BASIC

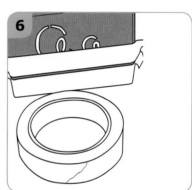

INSTRUCTIONS

1 Apply two coats of Graphite chalk paint to the outer sides of the boxes using a natural bristle brush, so the fabric is covered completely. (Paint the bottoms and insides if desired.) Allow the paint to dry completely; this will take an hour or two, depending on humidity.

2 Spritz the back of the stencils with low-tack adhesive and allow it to dry. Center a stencil on the side of a box and pat it into place. Alternatively, you can secure the stencil in place with painter's tape.

3 Load the stencil brush with a tiny amount of Old White chalk paint.

4 Remove excess paint onto a folded paper towel by swirling the brush onto it.

5 Holding one hand inside the box to support the side being stenciled, gently apply the paint into the openings of the stencil, redipping the brush as necessary. Remove the stencil.

6 Using painter's tape and following the construction lines on the box, mask off thin stripes running the horizontal length of the box, above and below the letters. Apply more Old White within those stripes to mimic the guidelines on an old-fashioned chalkboard. Allow the paint to dry thoroughly.

PLAY FURNITURE

Designed by: Charlotte Rivers

The **LÄTT** table and chair set can be turned into something really special, simply by using some paint and fabric. Adding a chalkboard top to the table will keep little ones entertained for hours, while the custom-made padded seats for the chairs will keep them comfy as they create.

MATERIALS

IKEA® HOME FURNISHINGS
LÄTT CHILDREN'S TABLE AND
2 X CHAIRS
WHITE, PINE $24.99

- **CHALKBOARD PAINT**
- **SANDPAPER**
- **PAINTER'S TAPE**
- **2 COLORS OF PAINT**
- **PAINTBRUSH**

- **2 PIECES OF FABRIC:**
  13¾ INCHES (35 CM) SQUARE
- **2 PIECES OF FOAM: 9 INCHES
  (23 CM) SQUARE**
- **DECOUPAGE GLUE/SEALER
  SUCH AS MOD PODGE**

TIME: 4–5 HRS
(INCLUDING DRYING TIME)
DIFFICULTY: INTERMEDIATE

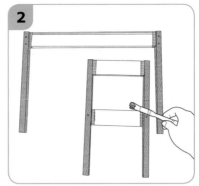

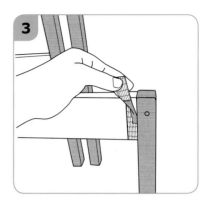

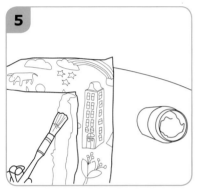

INSTRUCTIONS

1 Begin by painting the unfinished underside of the tabletop, which will become the top side, with chalkboard paint. You will need to give it about three coats of paint. Allow it to dry in between coats, and sand each time to help the paint adhere.

2 Before any assembly, lay out and tape up the edges of the middle sections of the outer frame of the table and chairs. Then paint the legs on both with one of your chosen paint colors (yellow here). Allow it to dry, and then paint a second coat.

3 Remove the tape, then apply new tape to the painted legs before painting the middle sections with the second paint color (gray here). Apply two coats and allow it to dry.

4 Assemble the table and chairs, following the assembly instructions, but remembering to assemble the table top upside down.

5 Make the chair seat pads. Lay the fabric face down and place the upholstery foam on top. Apply decoupage glue/sealer around the edge of the foam and onto the fabric.

6 Fold the fabric up and around the foam, applying extra glue/sealer where necessary.

7 Apply the glue/sealer to both the chair seats and the underside of each pad, then secure the pads onto the seats.

HACK HINT: Fix a handle to the side of the table to hang a tub on for storing chalk.

TREE SWING

Designed by: Jenni Juurinen

Take the well-loved **FROSTA** stool and turn it into a fun swing. As well as hanging the swing outdoors during the summer, you could also bring it indoors during the winter months.

MATERIALS

IKEA® HOME FURNISHINGS **FROSTA** STOOL YELLOW, $19.99

- **SANDPAPER**
- **WHITE AND BLACK SPRAY PAINT, OR OTHER PAINT SUITABLE FOR OUTDOORS**
- **RULER**
- **PEN**
- **PAINTER'S TAPE**
- **POWER DRILL AND 7/8-INCH (22-MM) DRILL BIT**
- **ROPE: APPROXIMATELY ¾ INCHES (2 CM) IN DIAMETER**

TIME: 2–3 HRS (INCLUDING DRYING TIME)
DIFFICULTY: INTERMEDIATE

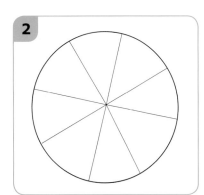

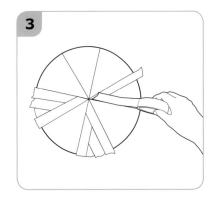

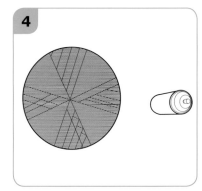

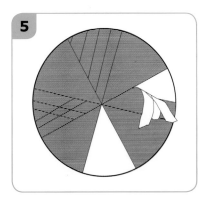

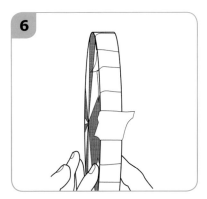

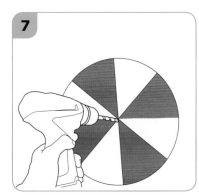

INSTRUCTIONS

1 Begin by using sandpaper to sand down the seat. Lay down newspaper to prepare an area outdoors for spray-painting and then spray-paint the seat white. Allow it to dry.

2 Using a ruler, or a straight edge, draw a line to divide the seat in half, then into four sections. Divide each section again into two, so you end up with eight sections.

3 Fill every second section with strips of the painter's tape, and also apply a strip of tape all the way around the edge.

4 Once you have finished applying the tape, spray-paint the seat again, this time using your black spray paint. Allow it to dry.

5 Remove all the tape from every other section to reveal the pattern.

6 Use small strips of the painter's tape to mask stripes around the edge of the seat, and spray-paint with black spray paint. Allow the seat to dry, and then remove the tape.

7 Drill a hole through the middle of the seat using a ⅞-inch (22-mm) drill bit. Pull the rope through the hole and make a big knot both under and above the seat to secure it in place.

BOOKSHELF DOLLHOUSE

Designed by: Charlotte Rivers

There is nothing better than a dollhouse for a kid's bedroom. This one can be made using the **STUVA** shelving unit frame as a base—it comes in two depths with this project using the narrower one—and adding a little extra medium-density fiberboard (MDF). Once ready, you can have fun filling it with figures and dollhouse furniture of your choice.

MATERIALS

IKEA® HOME FURNISHINGS
STUVA SHELVING UNIT FRAME
WHITE, DEPTH 11¾ INCHES (30 CM), $29.99

IKEA® HOME FURNISHINGS
2 X **STUVA GRUNDLIG** SHELF
WHITE, $5.00

- **MEDIUM-DENSITY FIBERBOARD (MDF):
  MEASURING 20½ X 1¼ INCHES (52 X 3 CM)
  FOR ROOF SECTION 1; MEASURING 20 X 1¼
  INCHES (51 X 3 CM) FOR ROOF SECTION 2;
  MEASURING 10¼ X 6 INCHES (26 X 15 CM)
  FOR TOP WALL; MEASURING 10¼ X 6½
  INCHES (26 X 16.5 CM) FOR MIDDLE WALL**
- **PENCIL**
- **DECORATIVE PAPER**
- **GLUE**
- **SCISSORS**
- **MASTIC GUN AND MASTIC**
- **POWER DRILL WITH SCREWDRIVER BIT**
- **5 ¼-INCH (5-MM) SCREWS**
- **PAINT**
- **PAINTBRUSH**
- **DOLLHOUSE FIGURES AND FURNITURE**

TIME: 6 HRS (INCLUDING DRYING TIME)
DIFFICULTY: INTERMEDIATE

2

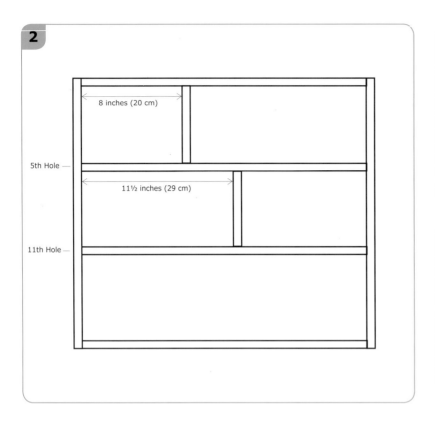

8 inches (20 cm)

5th Hole

11½ inches (29 cm)

11th Hole

3

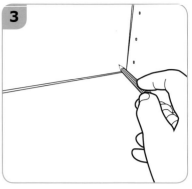

4

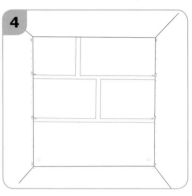

INSTRUCTIONS

1 Begin by putting the **STUVA** shelving unit together following the assembly instructions.

2 Position the shelves at levels 5 and 11, measuring from the top down. Position the top and middle walls at 8 inches (20 cm) in from the left, and 11½ inches (29 cm) in from the left, respectively.

3 Use a pencil to mark out the shapes of the rooms on the back panel of the shelving unit. This will give you the size guide you need for cutting the "wallpaper."

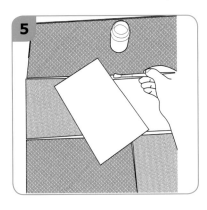

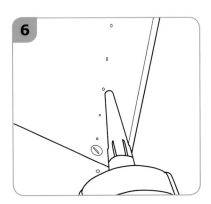

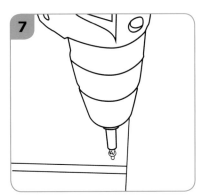

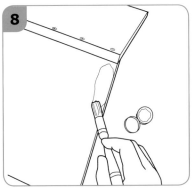

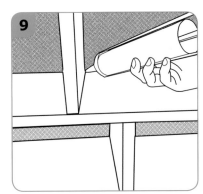

4 Remove the walls and shelves to reveal your pencil marks. Lay your decorative papers over these shapes and cut them to size.

5 You can now secure your wallpaper to the back panel of each room using glue. Allow them to dry.

6 Use mastic to fill the holes down each inside panel of the shelving unit.

7 Now drill holes and screw the two roof sections together. To do this place the larger piece of MDF (section 1) at the end of the shorter piece of MDF (section 2) to form a 90-degree angle.

8 Now paint the roof and the dividing walls. Here, the roof is painted red and the dividing walls white. Give everything two coats of paint and allow them to dry.

9 Glue the two dividing walls in place and secure at the top and bottom on both sides with mastic. Place the roof on the house, and fill it with furniture and dolls.

WINDOW SEAT

Designed by: Elyse Major

Transform a garden bench into a colorful and comfy window seat to decorate any room in your house. Pile it high with cozy pillows and store your books and magazines on the handy lower shelf. Any model of bench can be used and painted in a color of your choice.

MATERIALS

IKEA® HOME FURNISHINGS **ÄPPLARÖ** BENCH BROWN-STAINED, $60.00

- **PINE SHELVING: 8 INCHES (20 CM) WIDE**
- **4 CONSTRUCTION SCREWS: #6, 1½ INCH (4 CM) LONG**
- **HACKSAW**
- **SANDPAPER**
- **PRIMER**
- **PAINT**
- **FOAM PAINT PAD AND/OR FLAT PAINTBRUSH**

TIME: 1 HR+
DIFFICULTY: INTERMEDIATE

INSTRUCTIONS

1 Assemble the bench following the assembly instructions. Add a shelf by cutting a piece of pine shelving to fit on top of the lower bench supports. Attach with #6 1½-inch (4-cm) construction screws.

2 Give all wood a light sanding and wipe away any dust.

> **HACK HINT:** The discontinued **NORDEN** bench was used to make the project as shown, but the same results can be achieved with the **ÄPPLARÖ** bench.

3 Apply a coat of primer to the entire piece using a paint pad or a flat paintbrush. Watch for drips as you paint between the slats of the bench. Allow it to dry.

4 Then paint the seat portion white and the lower portion a cherry red. Allow it to dry and repeat until you have the desired richness of application.

5 Once the painted bench has completely dried, top with a few pillows.

ROLLING COOLER

Designed by: Charlotte Rivers

This dual-function project is great for the summer. It sees the **SILVERÅN** bathroom storage bench transformed into a rolling drinks cooler and seat, perfect for a summer barbecue. The inside of the bench is lined with polystyrene foam sheets to keep bottles and cans chilled, and the top of the bench is padded for comfort.

MATERIALS

IKEA® HOME FURNISHINGS **SILVERÅN** STORAGE BENCH LIGHT BROWN, $69.99

- **PENCIL AND RULER**
- **SAW**
- **CRAFT KNIFE TO CUT POLYSTYRENE FOAM SHEETS TO SIZE**
- **POLYSTYRENE FOAM SHEETS: 2 SIDES MEASURING 16 X 13 INCHES (40.5 X 33 CM); 2 ENDS MEASURING 10¼ X 13 INCHES (26 X 33 CM); BASE MEASURING 18¼ X 10½ INCHES (46.5 X 26.5 CM); TOP MEASURING 18 X 13 INCHES (46 X 33 CM)**
- **MASTIC GUN AND MASTIC**
- **CLOTH**
- **4 LIGHT DUTY SWIVEL BEARING CASTERS: 1⅝ INCHES (4 CM) AND MOUNTING SCREWS**
- **POWER DRILL AND ⅜-INCH (10-MM) DRILL BIT**
- **GLUE**
- **FOAM: 14 X 21¼ INCHES (35.5 X 54 CM)**
- **FABRIC: 27½ X 20 INCHES (70 X 51 CM)**
- **STAPLE GUN AND STAPLES**

TIME: 3 HRS
DIFFICULTY: INTERMEDIATE

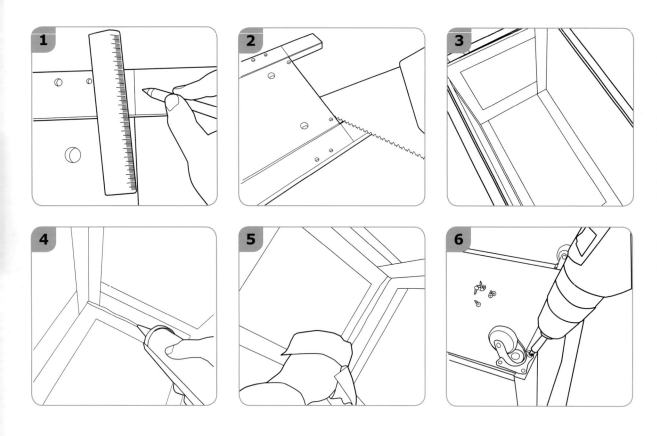

INSTRUCTIONS

1 Begin by attaching the four legs to the two sides of the storage bench, following the assembly instructions. Then use a pencil and ruler to mark a line on each of the legs, in line with the base of the sides on all four legs.

2 Saw the bottom part of all four legs off, and then continue to assemble the storage box following the assembly instructions.

3 Slide the two 16 x 13 inch (40 x 33 cm) polystyrene foam side sheets into the box, then the two 10¼ x 13 inch (26 x 33 cm) end pieces, and lastly the 18¼ x 10½ inch (46.5 x 26.5 cm) base piece.

4 Use mastic to seal all the joins around the base and in each of the four corners of the polystyrene foam. To do this, first squirt the mastic out of its tube using a mastic gun.

5 Then use a damp cloth and your finger to smooth the mastic along and press it gently into the grooves. Allow it to dry.

6 Next, attach the four casters onto the corners of the box with a screwdriver and the included screws. Be sure all casters are installed to face the same direction.

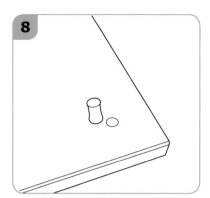

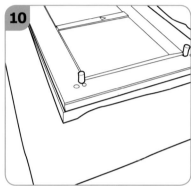

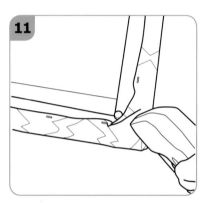

7 Move on to the lid. As we have inserted polystyrene foam into the inside of the box, you will need to make new holes for the little knobs that hold the lid in place. To do this, measure ¼ inch (5 mm) in diagonally toward the middle of your box from the existing hole. Mark with a pencil and then drill using a ⅜-inch (10-mm) drill bit.

8 Place the four knobs into your newly drilled holes.

9 Center and glue your top polystyrene foam sheet on the bottom of the lid. Allow it to dry.

10 Lay your fabric out on a flat surface, lay the polystyrene foam on top, and then place the lid on top of that.

11 Pull the fabric up and over to the inside of the lid. Make a small fold so you have a neat edge, and then use your staple gun to secure the fabric to the inside of the lid.

HACK HINT: If the little knobs that hold the lid in place do not sit snugly in your newly drilled holes, you could always secure them in place with some wood glue.

MINI KITCHEN

Designed by: Jane Hughes

This little play kitchen has a removable stove top, so can still be used as a stool when needed. The pegboard is great for hanging pots and pans and the little gingham step can be used as a picnic table. The handle for dish towels, hangers for cups, and potholders add a realistic finishing touch, while the curtain hides the equipment away when not in use.

MATERIALS

IKEA® HOME FURNISHINGS **BEKVÄM** STEP STOOL
WHITE, $19.99

- **PAINT: YELLOW, WHITE, BLACK**
- **PAINTBRUSHES**
- **PRECUT PEGBOARD: 9½ X 14¼ INCHES (24 X 36 CM)**
- **6 SMALL WOOD SCREWS**
- **SCREWDRIVER**
- **SEWING MACHINE**
- **2 PIECES OF PLAIN UPHOLSTERY-WEIGHT FABRIC: 10¼ X 15 INCHES (26 X 38 CM)**
- **IRON AND IRONING BOARD**
- **FELT: AT LEAST 10 INCHES (25 CM) SQUARE**
- **RIC RAC TRIMS OR SIMILAR: 40 INCHES (1 M)**
- **VELCRO (HOOK AND LOOP TAPE) 8 INCHES (20 CM) LONG**
- **BLACK ELECTRICAL TAPE**
- **DOWEL: ⅛ INCH (3 MM) IN DIAMETER, APPROXIMATELY 6½ INCHES (16 CM) LONG**
- **CRAFT KNIFE**
- **SMALL JAR LID**
- **WHITE PAPER**
- **STRONG GLUE**
- **SMALL METAL HANDLE**
- **5 SMALL WOODEN KNOBS**
- **3 PLASTIC SELF-ADHESIVE HOOKS**
- **GINGHAM SELF-ADHESIVE PLASTIC/VINYL**
- **PATTERNED FABRIC: 13 X 10¼ INCHES (33 X 26 CM)**
- **PLASTIC COATED CURTAIN WIRE: 14 INCHES (35.5 CM), PLUS 2 HOOKS AND 2 EYES (FOR FITTING)**
- **THREAD, PINS, SCISSORS, CRAFT KNIFE, PENCIL, PEN, RULER, AND WIRE CUTTERS (FOR CURTAIN WIRE)**

TIME: 1 DAY
DIFFICULTY: INTERMEDIATE

HACK HINT: Do check that your dowel will fit snugly into the pegboard holes, as these may vary in size.

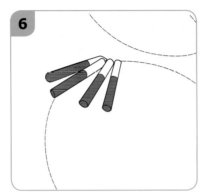

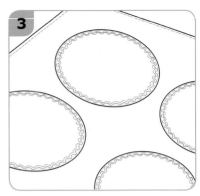

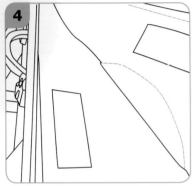

INSTRUCTIONS

1 Assemble the stool following the assembly instructions, and paint it in the colors as shown, or in your chosen colors.

2 Paint the pegboard white and allow it to dry. Attach the pegboard securely to the back top edge of the stool using four small wood screws.

3 To make the stove top, take the fabric pieces and place right side together. Using a ³⁄₈-inch (1-cm) seam allowance, sew around three sides, leaving one side open for turning. Turn the right way round and topstitch the remaining side closed. Press. From the felt, cut out four circles, each 4 inches (10 cm) in diameter. Pin the circles in place and stitch down. Sew on the ric rac trim around the edges.

4 Cut the Velcro into four pieces, each measuring 2 inches (5 cm) long. Stick a hook piece to each of the four corners of the reverse side of stove top; stick the corresponding loop piece to each corner on the top of the stool.

5 Attach the stove top to the stool. Take the black electrical tape and place around the sides and front of the top step.

6 Use a craft knife to cut the dowel into four lengths each measuring 1⁵⁄₈ inch (4 cm) long. Paint the ends and allow them to dry.

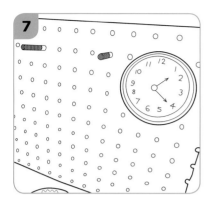

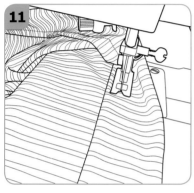

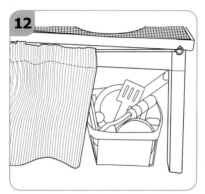

7 When the paint is dry, push the dowels firmly into the pegboard holes. Take the jar lid, trace around the shape and cut out a circle in white paper. Draw on a clock face and stick inside the lid. Attach this to the pegboard using strong glue.

8 Attach the metal handle to the side of the stool using the remaining two small wood screws.

9 Paint the wooden knobs, and when dry, glue four along the front of the stool and one at the side. Add the self-adhesive hooks to the underside of the top step, for hanging cups onto.

10 Take the self-adhesive plastic or vinyl and trace the shape of the lower step. Neatly cut it out and stick down in place.

11 Take the patterned fabric and fold over one of the longer edges to make a 1⅝-inch (4-cm) deep hem. Stitch down (this will make the channel for the curtain wire to pass through). Press.

12 Twist the hooks into each end of the curtain wire. The eyes should be screwed into the front of the lower step in a position that keeps the curtain wire taut. Push the curtain wire through the channel at the top of the curtain and hook each end onto the eyes to hang the curtain.

PLAYHOUSE

Designed by: Jenni Juurinen

The **KURA** bed is a really versatile bed and this clever modification makes it even better with the addition of a play area using plywood. It would make a great addition to a child's bedroom for hours of imaginative play.

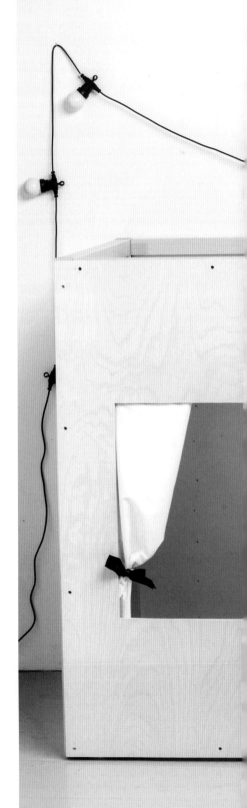

MATERIALS

IKEA® HOME FURNISHINGS **KURA** REVERSIBLE BED WHITE/PINE, $209.00

- **PLYWOOD: 2 END PIECES MEASURING 38½ X 45¼ INCHES (98 X 115 CM); WINDOW PIECE MEASURING 29½ X 45¼ INCHES (75 X 115 CM); FRONT PIECE MEASURING 35 X 12½ INCHES (89 X 32 CM)**
- **BLACK CHALKBOARD PAINT**
- **PAINT ROLL**
- **PENCIL**
- **RULER**
- **PIERCING SAW**
- **SANDPAPER**
- **PAINTER'S TAPE**
- **BLACK FURNITURE PAINT**
- **PAINTBRUSH**
- **POWER DRILL**
- **30 2-INCH (5-CM) SCREWS**

TIME: 6 HRS
DIFFICULTY: ADVANCED

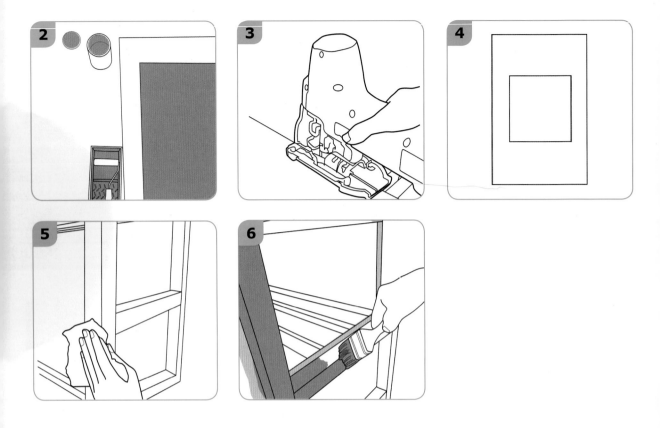

INSTRUCTIONS

1 Begin by assembling the **KURA** bed, following the assembly instructions.

2 Next, take your plywood (which can be pre-cut at your local hardware store), paint one of the 38½ x 45¼-inch (98 x 115-cm) end pieces on one side with black chalkboard paint and allow it to dry. This will become the outside of one end.

3 Take your 29½ x 45¼-inch (75 x 115-cm) window panel and mark out a 17 x 18-inch (43 x 46-cm) window in the center using your pencil and ruler. Cut out the window shape using your piercing saw.

4 Sand the edges afterward, if needed, so that the window frame has a smooth edge.

5 Sand the stairs of the bed to get them ready for painting.

6 Mask with painter's tape the areas around the stairs and paint the stairs with black furniture paint with the paintbrush. Allow it to dry.

HACK HINT: To achieve a more colorful look, you can paint the plywood panels too, choosing bright primary colors.

7

1 Front Piece
35 x 12½ inches
(89 x 32 cm)

2 End Pieces
38½ x 45¼ inches
(98 x 115 cm)

1 Window Piece
29½ x 45¼ inches
(75 x 115 cm)

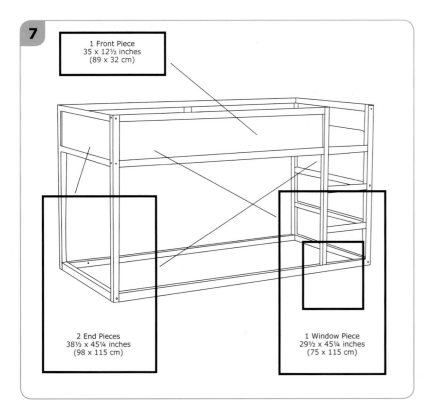

8

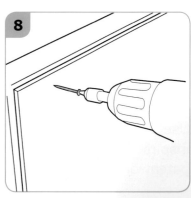

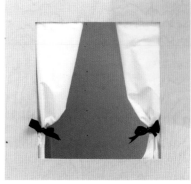

7 You are now ready to attach the plywood to the bed. Study the plan to make sure you are attaching the plywood in the correct places. Once you are ready, decide which end you'd like the chalkboard panel to be, and attach that end piece first using your drill and screws. Ensure that the chalkboard painted side is facing out.

HACK HINT: You can make simple curtains from two pieces of fabric by stapling them to the back of the plywood above the window aperture.

8 You can now attach all the other pieces of plywood using your drill and screws. (Note: the end pieces are both attached to the *outside* of the bed frame.)

COVERED SOFA

Designed by: Pernilla Frazier

Make a loveseat worthy of its name!
Use a favorite textile as your design
inspiration and fashion a fabulous
patchwork using high-end remnants.

MATERIALS

IKEA® HOME FURNISHINGS **EKTORP** LOVESEAT
VARIOUS COLORS, NORDVALLA GRAY
SHOWN HERE, $479.00

- **ASSORTED FABRIC REMNANTS FROM KREATELIER.COM**
- **DECORATIVE TEXTILE (2 ANTHROPOLOGIE DISH TOWELS SHOWN)**
- **SEAM RIPPER**
- **TAPE MEASURE**
- **SCISSORS**
- **PINS**
- **SEWING MACHINE**

TIME: 1 HR+
DIFFICULTY: ADVANCED

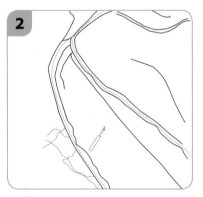

INSTRUCTIONS

1 Gather an assortment of remnant fabrics in the same color scheme. You will need sturdier fabrics for the seat cushions. Spread out all fabric to determine how to best combine it. For this project, one panel of each cushion will be transformed into a mixed patterned patchwork, framed by the solid rest of the original slipcover (which, for the sake of clarity, is shown as white in the diagrams). However, you may wish to do all sides; the choice is yours!

2 Start by carefully loosening the panels of each top side with a seam ripper. You will need to use scissors on the back cushions only, to cut 4 inches (10 cm) above the zipper.

HACK HINT: For best results, use fabrics made for upholstery purposes for the seat cushions.

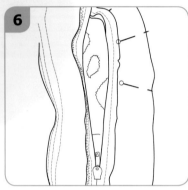

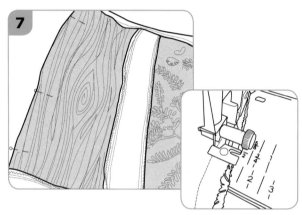

3 Next, use sharp scissors to cut one large insert from each cushion (back cushion shown), taking care to keep zippers and piping intact. Set aside the cutouts to use as templates for creating the patchwork panels.

4 Stitch together the mixed patches, allowing for a ½-inch (1.2-cm) seam allowance. Connect using a straight-stitch along the back, followed by topstitch on the face to make the seam extra strong (if your chosen fabrics fray easily, finish the patchwork seams with zigzag stitching). Make the patchwork rectangles slightly larger than the templates.

5 Put each template on top of each patchwork panel and cut around it to get the same size, except on the bottom of the back cushions, where 1 inch (2.5 cm) needs to be added for the seam allowance.

6 Turn the original cushion cover inside-out and pin on the new front, with the right side down to the cushion.

7 Sew from the back of the original cushion cover side, following the existing piping seam with a zipper foot. It is important to remember to keep the zipper open a little, otherwise you won't be able to turn the cover to the right side! Use a zigzag stitch all the way around. Turn out each cushion cover, and re-cover the cushions.

ROCKING CHAIR

Designed by: Audrey Smit

This is a great way to turn the classic **SUNDERÖ** outdoor chair into a delightful rocking chair, ideal for your deck or backyard.

MATERIALS

IKEA® HOME FURNISHINGS **SUNDERÖ**
OUTDOOR CHAIR
GRAY-STAINED, $130.00

- **ROCKING CHAIR RUNNERS**
- **RULER OR LEVEL**
- **PEN**
- **MINI SAW OR JAPANESE SAW**
- **SCREWDRIVER AND HAMMER**
- **SANDPAPER**
- **POCKET HOLE JIG KIT**
- **POCKET HOLE SCREWS: ¾ INCH (2 CM) LONG**
- **POWER DRILL**
- **WOOD GLUE**
- **PAINTBRUSH**
- **PRIMER**
- **PAINT**

TIME: 3 HRS
DIFFICULTY: ADVANCED

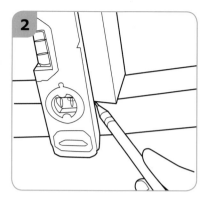

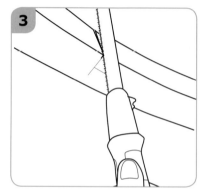

INSTRUCTIONS

1 Assemble the chair following the assembly instructions. To work out where to place your assembled chair on the rocking chair runners, place the runners under the chair and leave about 8½ inches (22 cm) on each end to center your chair.

2 Place a ruler or level against the legs of the chair to trace where you need to cut the wood at the right angle. Trace the incision to go about ¾–1 inch (2–2.5 cm) deep into the wood.

3 With a mini saw or Japanese saw, cut the part of the wood you just traced. This will be where the legs of the chair will be positioned.

HACK HINT: Any outdoor chair with arm rests would be suitable for this project, such as the **ÄPPALARÖ**, **FALSTER**, and **ÄNGSÖ** armchairs from IKEA® home furnishings.

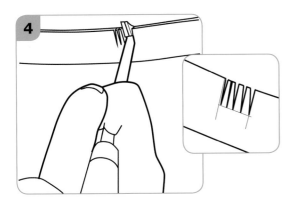

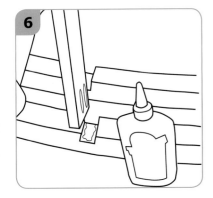

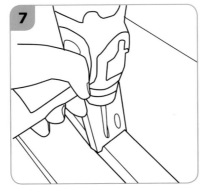

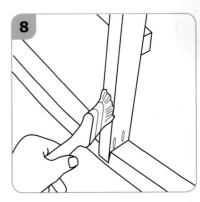

4 Make several dents across the runner and remove the pieces with a screwdriver and hammer. Sand down any leftover bits of wood. The chair should fit in snuggly.

5 Using the pocket hole jig kit, drill two pocket holes in the back of each leg of the chair. For the **SUNDERÖ** chair, you should set up the drill bit and jig for ¾ wood stock and set the jig on the fourth stop.

6 Apply wood glue along the rocking runner dents and place the chair legs into the dents.

7 Clean off any excess glue and drill in the pocket hole screws. Allow the glue to dry for 24 hours.

8 Sand the chair and runner, apply a coat of primer and then paint in the colors of your choice. You will need at least two or three coats for best results.

HACK HINT: If you are looking for a shortcut for this project, simply paint the runners in a fun, contrasting color and leave the chair itself unpainted.

OUTDOOR FLOOR CUSHION

Designed by: Charlotte Rivers

This outdoor floor cushion has been created using three long-lasting **SIGNE** rugs, making it ideal for outdoor use, either in your garden or backyard. The rugs are machine washable and so are easy to keep clean. A pair would work well together, so two could be made at the same time using different colored rugs.

MATERIALS

3 X IKEA® HOME FURNISHINGS **SIGNE** RUGS ASSORTED COLORS, $3.99 EACH

- **QUILT RULER**
- **PENCIL**
- **SCISSORS**
- **TAPE MEASURE**
- **PINS**
- **SEWING MACHINE**
- **FILLER**

TIME: 4 HRS
DIFFICULTY: ADVANCED

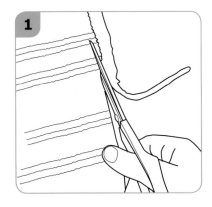

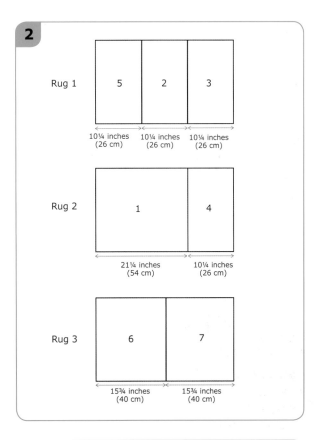

INSTRUCTIONS

1 As the rugs aren't exactly straight, take your quilt ruler and draw a straight line at the edges of each of the rugs. To ensure the line is straight, line up the top of your quilt ruler with the top end of the rug. Then cut these edges off—this will include the tassels and the sewn secured edge—to give you three neat, rectangular pieces of "fabric."

2 Now you are ready to measure out the different sections of fabric that you will need. Take your first rug and measure three 10¼-inch (26-cm) wide sections and cut—these will form three of your sides. Take the second rug and measure one 21¼-inch (54-cm) square and one 10¼-inch (26-cm) section and cut—this is your fourth side and your top. Take your third rug and cut it in half—this will be your base. You should have seven pieces of fabric in total.

3 Lay all the pieces of fabric out, right side down on a flat surface, as shown in the diagram.

HACK HINT: If choosing an alternative rug for this project, do make sure that it is not too thick, otherwise you will have difficulty sewing the pieces together.

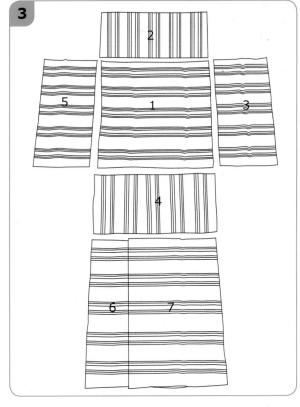

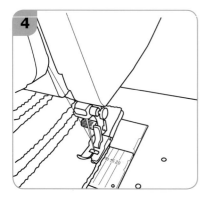

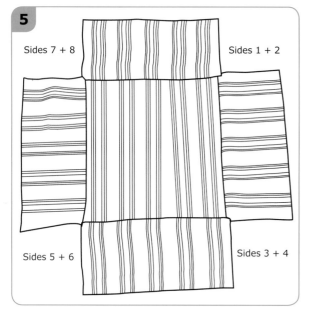

Sides 7 + 8

Sides 1 + 2

Sides 5 + 6

Sides 3 + 4

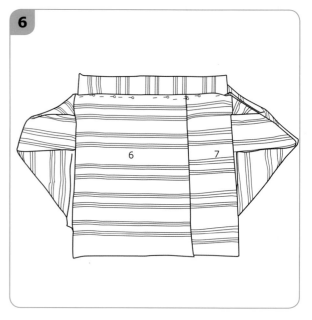

4 Using your sewing machine, begin by sewing section 1 to section 2. Then sew section 3 to section 1. Then sew section 4 to section 1. Then sew section 5 to section 1. Ensure you match up the edges of each section and sew a ³⁄₈ inch (1 cm) seam allowance.

5 Next, you will need to sew all the sides together. Start with sides 1 and 2, and then move on to 3 and 4, then 5 and 6, then 7 and 8. As you go, ensure that you are sewing all your seams in the right direction, i.e., they should all face inside the cushion.

6 Making sure that the sewn section is inside out, pin your two base sections (6 and 7) to the sewn section. You are creating an envelope back, meaning that the two sections of fabric that make up the base will overlap, and this is how the filler in the floor cushion will remain inside. Pin one side to the sewn section and sew onto the base. Repeat for all four sides of the base section.

7 Turn your cushion the right way out and stuff with filler.

SUPPLIERS

Anthropologie
anthropologie.com
Dish towels

Cath Kidston
www.cathkidstonUSA.com
www.cathkidston.com
Fabric

Chic Mouldings
chicmouldings.com
Decorative resin appliqués

Fabric.com
fabric.com
Laminated fabric, fabric

Home Depot
homedepot.com
*Casters, chicken wire, latex paint,
spray paint, porch handle, tools*

Janeen D. Chabot
Pinterest: JaneenDChabot
DIY projects

Jo-Ann Fabrics
joann.com
Fabric glue, foam, trimming

Kreatelier
kreatelier.com
Home decorator fabrics

Michaels
michaels.com
*German glass glitter, acrylic paint,
acrylic coating spray, fusible webbing,
glue, supplies*

Peony and Sage
peonyandsage.com
Fabric

Sea Rose Cottage
searosecottage.com
Annie Sloan products, hardware

DESIGNERS

Nancy Chace
searosecottage.com

Rachel Denbow
smileandwave.typepad.com

Sarah M. Dorsey
sarahmdorseydesigns.blogspot.com

Danielle Driscoll
findingsilverpennies.com

Pernilla Frazier
kreatelier.com

Jane Hughes
teawagontales.blogspot.com

Stephanie Jones
www.mrsjonespaintedfinishes.com

Jenni Juurinen
jennijuurinen.com

Elyse Major
tinkeredtreasures.com

Jessica Mayhall
www.creativefinishesstudios.com

Stacey Remiker-Flesch
cottagestitches.com

Charlotte Rivers
charlotterivers.com

Audrey Smit
thislittlestreet.com/blog

INDEX